We know that our patchwork heritage is a strength, not a weakness.

—*Barack Obama*

Inaugural address, January 20, 2009

Journey of Hope

Quilts Inspired by President Barack Obama

Carolyn L. Mazloomi

Foreword by Meg Cox, president of
the Alliance for American Quilts

Voyageur Press

long march of
rch for a m
ng and mo
r the pres
e I believe
enges of
- unless w
that we m
mmon hop
e same a
place, but we a
- towards a bett
r grandchildren
newfound power
REALIZE THE VISION
Celebrating Cultural Diversity
Now is the time
NO LIMIT.
one smart move
created equal
STOP THE NONSENSE AND GO WITH THE LEADER
New energy
AUTHENTICITY
above ordinary
People will stare
A new range of possibilities
FOCUS
Are you ready
WORLD CHANGING.
only the beginning.
INSPIRATION
It's amazing
We Can Do It!
Future
THE PRESIDENT
Innovation.
optimistic
proactive and prepared
calm
Fresh ideas
YOUR WAKE UP CALL.
Different Standards
Smart
Capable
innovative
creative
Inspiration
strong
Soulful
Alternatives
WECHSELN
Reliable.
ON TRACK
CAN DO.
Another Look
distinctively better
CREATE A LASTING LEGACY.
Flat out wonderful
Die Zukunft bauen
STRONG · FOCUSED · SAFE
'miracle'
dream
Wisdom
Believe
peace
NEXT GENERATION
Awaken Your Soul
new day
ambitious
A triumph of principle over color
The best advice is to plan ahead.
GREAT OPPORTUNITY
YOUR CHOICE
Believe
A new way to think smart
Anticipation
New. Idealist
BE THE CHANGE
INSPIRED
big difference.
EXTRAORDINARY
Inspiring
Dream
challenges
Über-sophisticated
Rethink American.
sense of hope
GOOD THINGS DO HAPPEN
created equal.
solutions
So many choices.
Keep Moving Forward
New Course
Winning
All Inclusive
The Future
Taking the Initiative
Get more done
Repair
WELCOME
Peace
big ideas
Finally...
Caring.
It Makes All The Difference.
ANSWERED
Ganz oben mitspielen
MAGIC
INSPIRED.
On the Right Track
Community Works
All are Welcome in America
PROMISES AND CHALLENGES
dream
TRUSTED NAME
ENOUGH SAID.
And they'll be counting on us for years to come.
Mann der Zukunft
Inspiring others to act
The Change Agent
The smart, silent type.
Respecting our proud tradition
RESTORE TRUST
You Can Count On.
Now More Than Ever
Obama and American anti-elitism
Your Success... Is Our Goal!
Take control.
IT'S A WORLD OF PERSPECTIVES.
The time is now.
LET THE GOOD TIMES ROLL
Great
Just what the world needs,
EVENT OF THE YEA
The picture is only half the story
MIND-BOGGLING
time will never be the same!
Today we push the standard
It loo
differe
working for you?
WHEN YOU'RE READY TO LIVE IT
United, not divided
Obama
Peace Is What We Need!
Focus
Changing America is up to all of us, not just Obama
change
IS IT POSSIBLE TO BE THIS PASSIONATE

On the front cover:
Main image: *Fearless* by Sherry Shine
Top row: *Journeys Begin from Home* by
Lauren Austin, *At Last* by Bisa Butler, *Winds for
Change* by Marion Coleman, *Blossom of Change*
by Cynthia Catlin, *Celebrating Barack Obama:
America's First Afro-American President* by
Viola Burley Leak, *In His Father's Village*
by Valerie C. White
Bottom row: *The Obama Streak of Lightening*
by Lynette S. Jackson, *Universal Matrix: The
Binding Force That Unites Us* by Mayota Hill,
Waves of Change by Kathy Zieben, *First Lady* by
Susan Shie, *The Journey: We Are the Ones We
Have Been Waiting For* by L'Merchie Frazier, *Free
Flowing* by Helen Murrell

On the spine:
Top: *It's a New Day!* by Debra Gabel
Bottom: *From Vision to Victory*
by Carolyn Crump

On the back cover:
Top row: *Black & White in a Red State* by
Sheryl Schleicher, *Obama Equals Hope* by
Jeanette Thompson, *Obama 44* by Jim Smoote,
Obamessiah by Penny Sisto, *Growing a
New America* by Barbara Ann McCraw,
Ain't Gonna Let Nobody Turn Me Around
by Carolyn L. Mazloomi
Bottom row: *Great Expectations* by Valerie
C. White, *44th President and First Lady* by
Diana Bracy, *Si se Puede! Dancing at the
Revolution* by Sabrina Zarco, *The Picture Is Only
Half the Story* by the Pixeladies (Deb Cashatt
and Kris Sazaki), *Obama* by Adrienne Yorinks,
One Vote Can Change the World by Bisa Butler

On the frontis: *The Journey: We Are the Ones
We Have Been Waiting For* by L'Merchie Frazier

On the title pages: *The Picture Is Only Half
the Story* by the Pixeladies (Deb Cashatt
and Kris Sazaki)

Editor: Margret Aldrich
Design Manager: LeAnn Kuhlmann
Designed by: Sarah Bennett
Cover designed by: Lois Stanfield

*To Rezvan, Damian, Farzad, and Farhad
for giving my life a sense of purpose and fulfillment.*

*And also to Kia, the sunshine of my life,
who married a good son and made him a better man.*

First published in 2010 by Voyageur Press, an imprint of MBI Publishing Company,
400 First Avenue North, Suite 300, Minneapolis, MN 55401 USA

Copyright © 2010 by Carolyn L. Mazloomi

Quilts copyright © 2010 by artists as noted

Love copyright © 2010 by Robert Indiana. Permission granted for use as a source of
artistic inspiration in *Election Results* by Laurie Brainerd. Lyrics from "Chocolate City"
© 1975 by George Clinton. Permission granted for use in *You Dig?* by Martha Gilbert.

The information in this book is true and complete to the best of our knowledge.
All recommendations are made without any guarantee on the part of the author or
Publisher, who also disclaims any liability incurred in connection with the use of this
data or specific details.

We recognize, further, that some words, model names, and designations mentioned
herein are the property of the trademark holder. We use them for identification
purposes only. This is not an official publication.

Voyageur Press titles are also available at discounts in bulk quantity for industrial or
sales-promotional use. For details write to Special Sales Manager at MBI Publishing
Company, 400 First Avenue North, Suite 300, Minneapolis, MN 55401 USA.

To find out more about our books, visit us online at www.voyageurpress.com.

ISBN-13: 978-0-7603-3935-0

Printed in China

Library of Congress Cataloging-in-Publication Data
Mazloomi, Carolyn.
 Journey of hope : quilts inspired by President Barack Obama / Carolyn L.
Mazloomi.— 1st ed.
   p. cm.
  ISBN 978-0-7603-3935-0 (plc)
  1. Quilts—United States—History—21st century—Themes, motives. 2. Obama,
Barack. 3. Presidents—United States—Election—2008. 4. Art—Political aspects—
United States—History—21st century. I. Title.
 NK9112.M368 2010
 746.460973'074—dc22
                                                    2009046159

Contents

7   **Foreword by Meg Cox**

8   **Introduction**

THE QUILTS

12   **Renee Allen**
*I Never Thought I Would Live
to See the Day!*

14   **Gwendolyn Aqui**
A New Day

16   **Lauren Austin**
Journeys Begin from Home

18   **Alice Beasley**
We Are a Nation

20   **Carol Beck**
A Dream Realized

22   **Sherry Boram**
Dawn

24   **Edward Bostick**
*Thurgood Marshall, Supreme Court
Justice*

26   **Diana Bracy**
44th President and First Lady

28   **Laurie Brainerd**
Election Results

30   **Julius J. Bremer**
My President

32   **Carole Richburg Brown**
Hear My Silent Song

34   **Wendell George Brown**
Crossroads: Now Is the Time

36   **Bisa Butler**
At Last

38   **Bisa Butler**
One Vote Can Change the World

40   **Denise M. Campbell**
*From Kenya to Kansas the World
Rejoices*

42   **Cynthia Catlin**
Blossom of Change

44   **Betty Coburn**
Obama Drafted for the NBA

46   **Marion Coleman**
Speaking of Women

48   **Marion Coleman**
Winds for Change

50   **Connie Condrell**
Light at the End of the Tunnel

52   **Donnette A. Cooper**
America at the Crossroads

54   **Carolyn Crump**
From Vision to Victory

56   **Carolyn Crump**
Michelle

58   **Adriene Cruz**
Warrior of Light Shield for Obama

60   **Eileen Doughty**
Freedom's Box

62   **Jacqueline Dukes**
Oahu, Ohana, Obama

64   **Ife Felix**
Change Has Come

66   **Deborah Fell**
And Then There Was Hope

68   **Fiber Artists for Obama**
Yes! We Can

70   **Michelle D. Flamer**
Next

72   **L'Merchie Frazier**
*The Journey: We Are the Ones
We Have Been Waiting For*

74   **Marjorie Diggs Freeman**
Yes We Can . . . and in My Lifetime

76   **Debra Gabel**
It's a New Day!

78   **Sandra German**
Reflecting on Our Victory

80   **Martha Gilbert**
You Dig?

82   **Valerie Goodwin**
African Burial Ground

84   **Myrah Green**
Children Dancin' at the Tree of Life

86   **Sandra Hankins**
Everybody's All American

88   **Carole Harris**
O + C = 44

90   **Peggie Hartwell**
Restoration

92   **Sylvia Hernandez**
American Dream

94   **Sylvia Hernandez**
Obama Hawaiian Style

96   **Mayota Hill**
*Universal Matrix: The Binding Force
That Unites Us*

98   **Janice E. Hobson**
Starburst II

100   **Lawana Holland-Moore**
Wildest Dreams

102   **Sonji Hunt**
The Path of Unyielding Hope

104   **Charlotte Hunter**
Gallery of Presidents

106   **Lynette S. Jackson**
The Obama Streak of Lightening

108   **Marla Jackson**
The Journey Forward

110   **Joy-Lily**
Help, Hope & Hallelujah!

112   **Niambi Kee**
O Is for Obama

114 **Peg Keeney**
We the People: Together We Can

116 **Gloria Kellon**
The Journey Ends

118 **Sharon Kerry-Harlan**
DIS

120 **Beverly Huggins Kirk**
Transcendence

122 **Anita Knox**
The Guardians

124 **Carol Krueger**
That Won

126 **Deborah Lacativa**
Hope Rising

128 **Viola Burley Leak**
Celebrating Barack Obama: America's First Afro-American President

130 **Viola Burley Leak**
Change, Exchange and Vision

132 **Cynthia Lockhart**
Mr. President

134 **Cynthia Lockhart**
Spirit of Victory

136 **Jeanne Marklin**
Lift Every Voice and Sing for Obama

138 **Gwen Maxwell-Williams**
Obama—The Promise

140 **Barbara Ann McCraw**
Growing a New America

142 **Harriette A. Meriwether**
In My Lifetime . . . A Path of Injustice, Accomplishments, and a Victory Declared

144 **Ed Johnetta Miller**
title?

146 **Helen Murrell**
At This Moment

148 **Helen Murrell**
Free Flowing

150 **Sandra Noble**
Obama Lights the World with Hope

152 **Charlotte O'Neal**
In the Shadow of Our Freedom

154 **Pixeladies (Deb Cashatt and Kris Sazaki)**
The Picture Is Only Half the Story

156 **Theresa D. Polley-Shellcroft**
Jacob's Ladder: The Opening of the Heart of America

158 **Keisha Roberts**
Tears for Water

160 **Sheryl Schleicher**
Black & White in a Red State

162 **Marlene O'Bryant Seabrook**
They Paved the Way

164 **Latifah Shakir**
Dream the Impossible Dream

166 **Carole Lyles Shaw**
War and Freedom: African American Veterans Hail the Commander in Chief #2

168 **Maria C. Shell**
Colors Unfurled (aka If Betsy Ross Had My Stash)

170 **Susan Shie**
First Lady

172 **Sherry Shine**
Chronicles of a Journey

174 **Sherry Shine**
Fearless

176 **Sherry Shine**
The 44th

178 **Penny Sisto**
Obamessiah

180 **Bonnie J. Smith**
Obama in Blue

182 **Louisa Smith**
Yes We Can

184 **Jim Smoote**
Obama 44

186 **Carole Gary Staples**
Inspired Change

188 **Carole Gary Staples**
Unparalleled Journey

190 **Maxine S. Thomas**
Barack Obama: Realizing the American Dream

192 **Rosalind Thomas**
In My Time

194 **Jeanette Thompson**
Obama Equals Hope

196 **Elizabeth Warner**
Together We Bridge the Divide

198 **Torreah Cookie Washington**
The Hope of a New Day Begun

200 **Valerie C. White**
Great Expectations

202 **Valerie C. White**
In His Father's Village

204 **Cleota Wilbekin**
Mama's Freedom Apron

206 **Sherise Marie Wright**
6 Hours

208 **Adrienne Yorinks**
Obama

210 **Sauda A. Zahra**
Keepers of Your Destiny

212 **Sabrina Zarco**
Si se Puede! Dancing at the Revolution

214 **Kathy Zieben**
Waves of Change

216 **Acknowledgments**

216 **About the Author**

Foreword by Meg Cox

I believe that when historians dig down to the level of citizen experience, they'll discover that quilts actually predicted the 2008 election. Leading up to election day, Obama quilts were everywhere in the quilt community, online, and in public venues, and McCain quilts were scarce. Before the International Quilt Festival, a big annual fall show in Houston that year, quiltmakers were invited to submit quilts to a "Patchwork Politics" exhibit: the quilts ran three-to-one in Obama's favor.

Ever since quilting began, the political campaigns and causes that have generated the most passion also inspired the most quilts. In an era when women couldn't express their political opinion in the ballot box, they often did so in fabric, sometimes using brightly colored silk campaign ribbons to embellish quilts in the nineteenth century. It was an equally fiery passion for a history-making candidate that inspired so many quiltmakers—men and women, black, white, and other—to express their feelings about Barack Obama in fabric in the twenty-first century.

Yes, passionate political quilts are sometimes negative in tone, and there was evidence of that in this election too. The Houston display of political quilts included several Bush-bashing quilts, and one about Bill Clinton's political adventures called *Good Willy, Bad Willy*. There was an especially vitriolic quilt called *Hillary's Defeat*, which seemed to consist entirely of jagged points.

You won't see Obama-bashing quilts within these pages, because that isn't what esteemed curator and quilt collector Carolyn Mazloomi found when she set out to document and study the explosion of Obama-themed quilts made during and after the election. When Mazloomi spread the word that she was looking for Obama quilts for a book, hundreds of quilts came to her, some in the form of digital images in e-mails, but also actual, physical quilts, piled high in the front hall of her Ohio home. Mazloomi hit a nerve; she unleashed a flood.

The 103 quilts she has selected amaze with their variety and their intensity. They range from the raw efforts of novices to the dazzling craftsmanship of trained fine artists. There are no bedcovers here, though there were plenty of utilitarian quilts made during the election, often featuring the familiar Obama campaign logo, which appears in just a few of the quilts in this book. These passionate declarations Mazloomi chose were meant for the walls, whether for museum or home consumption, and not for beds. They belong in the public sphere, making collective commentary. There are quilts here that make us chuckle, others full of joy and celebration, and many that ask us to think hard about the past and the future. In general, these Obama quilts are more mindful of the moment than worshipful of the man. All are deeply personal.

Clearly this was not what Obama had in mind when he spoke of America's "patchwork heritage" in his inaugural address. But these quilts are likely to become among the most colorful and poignant of historical mementoes remarking on his election's significance. We have Carolyn Mazloomi to thank for gathering, sharing, and preserving them for the ages.

Meg Cox is a journalist, author, and quilter whose most recent book is The Quilter's Catalog: A Comprehensive Resource Guide *(Workman Publishing, 2008). A former staff writer for the* Wall Street Journal, *Cox is president of the nonprofit Alliance for American Quilts. She is a columnist for several national quilt publications and can be reached through her website, www.megcox.com.*

Introduction

The equality envisioned by the Declaration of Independence was far from a reality for all America's citizens. Slave ships arrived on the shores of North America more than three hundred years ago, and since that time African Americans have struggled to find their place on the canvas that is America. When the struggle for freedom continued in the late 1950s, the individuals participating in the civil rights movement could not have possibly foreseen that their protest in support of basic human dignity would culminate in a black man becoming commander-in-chief of the most powerful country on earth.

The election of 2008 has become one of the most defining moments in the political history of the United States and has successfully willed into being a world that could once only be imagined. From the moment Barack Obama was declared president, there were exclamations by my friends and innumerable Americans, "I never thought I'd live to see the day!" There was not one person or singular action that led to Obama's election. Instead, it was the collective struggle and leadership of generations of Americans, black and white, which led to the dismantling of segregation and institutional racism in the United States. If not for the determination and conviction of his predecessors, change in America could not have been possible.

Many hours before polls opened, lines started forming in the predawn light, people anxious to participate in the culmination of an election campaign that had captivated the world. Some people managed, in the words of Dr. Martin Luther King Jr., to judge Barack Obama by the "content of his character and not the color of his skin." For this one particular day Americans seemingly embraced the notion that we "are all endowed with certain unalienable rights." Obama's victory was, at once, sweeping and historic. For many Americans of all races and ethnicities, it suggested the healing of the legacy of slavery which had prohibited African Americans from fully participating as equal members of society, and offered the prospect of restoring the country's respect around the world. Equally important was the fact that the election allowed a new generation of young people to realize their enormous potential by imagining a world where their dreams actually can come true, and the possibilities for advancement are unlimited.

President Obama has the presence, principles, and disposition reflecting the qualities of a great American leader. His humility is seen as strength of character and vision. After his historic U.S. victory, Barack Obama's supporters exploded into song and dance around the world, from the streets of London, Havana, Paris, Berlin, and Sydney to a sleepy village in Kenya, to the small town of Obama in Japan. Americans positioned around the world poured into the streets to celebrate new hope and change. Many people feel Obama is America's opportunity for reconciliation globally.

In his January 20, 2009, inaugural address, President Barack Obama referenced America's "patchwork heritage." Little did he know how much he inspired the nation's quiltmakers. Quilting, present in this country since its establishment, has long been recognized as an important facet of our history. Quilts are recognized by historians as social and cultural documents representing the lives, values, and environments of their creators. The tradition of quilters using their artistic skills to commemorate historic moments is a long and continuing one.

Artists featured in *Journey of Hope: Quilts Inspired by President Barack Obama* are a multiethnic, multicultural, and multigenerational group moved by Obama's campaign and vision to mark the occasion with a commemorative quilt. Each quilt is a highly personal statement and a reflection of their shared experience as American citizens participating in the electoral process. They used a variety of techniques, including piecing, painting, appliqué, embroidery, dyeing, photography, beading, and digital transfer. Some quilts depict aspects of the Obama family's life stories and others connect their lives to the expansive sweep of American and African history and the civil rights movement. The quilts also express the joy and hope that many feel over Americans having elected its first African American president.

News of quilters making Obama quilts spread over the Internet on blogs and quilters' websites, and quilts were brought to show-and-tell at guilds. Curators began to organize exhibitions of Obama quilts. Art quilter and Obama campaign worker Dr. Sue Walen was among the first to showcase Obama quilts. Dr. Walen conceived of the exhibit when she was removing an Obama quilt she made from the Obama campaign offices in Bethesda. She wondered how many others had created quilts featuring Obama and his family. Walen put out a call for quilts, and within one day more than forty artists from across the country responded. Walen was able to find a space to exhibit the quilts in Bethesda, Maryland, at the Morris and Gwendolyn Cafritz Foundation Arts Center at Montgomery College's Takoma Park/Silver Spring Campus, and she produced a catalogue of the exhibit.

Folklorist and photodocumenter Roland L. Freeman, whose career began during the civil rights movement, was also inspired to curate an exhibition to celebrate Barack Obama's election. He enlisted my help in finding quilts for the exhibition, and I called on the members of Women of Color Quilters Network to participate. *Quilts for Obama: Celebrating the Inauguration of our 44th President* opened at the Historical Society of Washington, DC in less than a month after invitations were issued to artists. Mr. Freeman described the genesis of this exhibit as follows:

On November 4th, I was glued to the television watching the election returns, as were millions in this country and around the world. When it was announced that Barack Obama was the president-elect of the United States, my emotions overwhelmed me. I could hardly speak. Then came the amazing images of worldwide jubilation. My mind drifted back to other seminal events that for me were just as emotionally life-changing: my participation in the voting rights march from Selma to Montgomery; the 1963 March on Washington and Dr. King's "I Have a Dream" speech; and my joining the Poor People's Campaign as a photographer to cover the Mule Train caravan as it traveled from Marks, Mississippi, to Washington, DC.

In my lifetime, I've known three black men whose messages of peace, love, and racial harmony profoundly moved the masses: Martin Luther King Jr., Nelson Mandela, and Barack Obama. King said, "We shall overcome"; Nelson Mandela forgave his oppressors; and now Barack Obama has inspired Americans and others around the world to come together for change for a better tomorrow.

Quilts also played a role in fundraising for the Obama campaign. New Jersey quiltmaker Lisa Shepard Stewart organized a group of quilters, Fiber Artists for Obama, and

Ain't Gonna Let Nobody Turn Me Around

Carolyn L. Mazloomi I West Chester, Ohio I 2008 I
41 x 34 inches (104 x 86 cm) I Commercial cotton, hand-dyed
cotton, rayon thread, African cloth I Collaged, raw-edge appliquéd,
and machine quilted I *Collection of Sharon Henderson* I *Photo by
Chas. E. and Mary B. Martin*

proceeded to raise more than $120,000 by the end of the presidential race.

The national movement of quilters making works inspired by President Obama caught the attention of Karen Musgrave, an Illinois quiltmaker, who co-chairs an oral history project, *Quilters' S.O.S.—Save Our Stories*, sponsored by the Alliance for American Quilts. After the election, Musgrave started interviewing the quilters to record and preserve the motivation behind them making quilts to celebrate Obama. These interviews are to be given to the Library of Congress.

Joining this cadre of quilts created to celebrate this enormous historical moment, there is arguably no more appropriate adjective than "righteous" to describe *Journey of Hope: Quilts Inspired by President Barack Obama*. This assembly of quilt artists has crafted for the world a stream of prayer cloths—quilts with the expressive, effective power of any fervent prayer. Visible through these quilts are prayers of healing, deliverance, hope, and protection. Ranging from poignantly abstract to grippingly realistic, the messages are unmistakable. Although quilters created work inspired by their own unique experiences, there are three recurring themes in many of the works: participation in the voting process, hope for a brighter future, and paying homage to freedom fighters in the fight for equality.

Laurie Brainerd's abstraction *Election Results* and Bisa Butler's commentary *One Vote Can Change the World* engage our sense of hope by valuing diverse individual contributions to a collectively anticipated outcome. The virtue of patience rings true as we witness hope embedded in willing determination to endure endless lines of expectant voters. Gwendolyn Aqui's *A New Day* celebrates the act of her beloved eighty-three-year-old grandmother voting for the very first time. One wonders how many citizens in those lines voted for the first time because hope was alive in them for the first time. In contrast, one contemplates how many citizens endured these historically inexhaustible lines because their hope resided in a different prayer of possibility—the prayer that perhaps after years of casting a single vote in a desire for change, this 2008 election could finally be the one to fulfill a lifetime of faithful participation in a democracy that had remained dormant for them, and so many others, for far too long.

Let's just take a moment to study the emotion expressed in Myrah Green's *Children Dancin' at the Tree of Life*. Now let's allow ourselves to absorb the hopes of the millions of disillusioned youth that come alive in this piece. As students of their world, through their artistic interpretations, Green and others have become our teachers. We have the choice to embrace the inspired wisdom we see before us, or to blindly move past the graffiti of the hopeful. It is a choice that can change a nation and a global society, or it is a choice than can keep us wandering in endless wilderness. But let us not forget—it is always our choice.

Recognizing the fact that President Obama stands on the shoulders of a long line of freedom fighters whose vision fashioned his national and global victory are Peggie L. Hartwell's quilt *Transformation*, Marlene Seabrook's *They Paved the Way*, L'Merchie Frazier's *We Are the Ones We Have Been Waiting For*, and Carolyn Crump's *Vision to Victory*. Such freedom fighters as Frederick Douglass and Harriet Tubman, Medger Evers and Sojourner Truth, Martin Luther King Jr. and Thurgood Marshal, and many others who made progress towards equality are praised on these quilts. Personally, I will always associate the election of 2008 with the 1965 Selma to Montgomery, Alabama, freedom march. On March 7, 1965, as nonviolent marchers neared the Edmund Pettus Bridge, they were tear-gassed, beaten, and their processional stopped by Alabama state police. This historic event, known as Bloody Sunday, resulted in the passage of the 1965 Voting Rights Act. The Voting Rights Act was the first step taken to assure that, throughout the nation, no person would be denied the right to vote on account of race or color. When I stepped into the voting booth to cast my vote for Mr. Obama, I felt as if I had walked across the John Pettus Bridge.

Donnette Cooper's quilt, *America at the Crossroads*, and Sabrina Zarco's *Si se Puede! Dancing at the Revolution* focus on our perennial challenge to reconcile the competing imperatives of race, gender, religion, class, nationality, and sexual identity as we struggle to realize the vision of "a more perfect union." The inclusion of racially diverse and ethnically identified children and young people and the acceptance of those different from ourselves in contemporary multiracial Western society remains an important academic concern. Now it appears there is a small window for openness in accepting all citizens.

Many of the quilters represented in Journey of Hope view their work as expressions of their faith and spiritual journeys. If the Obama family hears echoes of clanking armor down the corridors of the White House, it is undoubtedly due, in part, to the fervent prayers of these quilters, as they gird up each Obama family member in spiritual armor during unceasing rituals of daily devotions. Their quilts are artistic representations of those devotional moments. Every step of President Obama's confident gait as he approaches another presidential challenge is a potent reminder of the prayer warriors who battle on his behalf—and, in the case of these warriors, with quilting needles poised.

Renee Allen

I Never Thought I Would Live to See the Day!

Throughout this historic election, a common sentiment expressed by many African Americans was, "I never thought I would live to see the day. . . ." Thus I was inspired to create my quilt *I Never Thought I Would Live to See the Day*.

The quilt depicts an elderly couple taking a stroll through a cemetery, populated by the many African Americans who witnessed many historic social and political changes. The headstones symbolize sacrifices made and lives lost in the name of freedom and equality for African American citizens from slavery to present day.

The headstones also honor some of the people who died in the pursuit of equality. The Emancipation Proclamation and the Voting Rights Act are also represented. The couple is smiling as they proudly hold an Obama campaign poster and an inauguration newspaper. They, too, never thought they would live to see the day when someone who looked like they do would hold the most powerful position in the free world—president of the United States of America.

I Never Thought I Would Live to See the Day!

Renee Allen I Ellenwood, Georgia I 2009 I 60 x 48 inches (152 x 122 cm) I Cotton, mud cloth, yarn, beads, acrylic paint I
Raw-edge machine appliquéd, hand appliquéd, machine quilted, and hand embellished I *Photo by Chas. E. and Mary B. Martin*

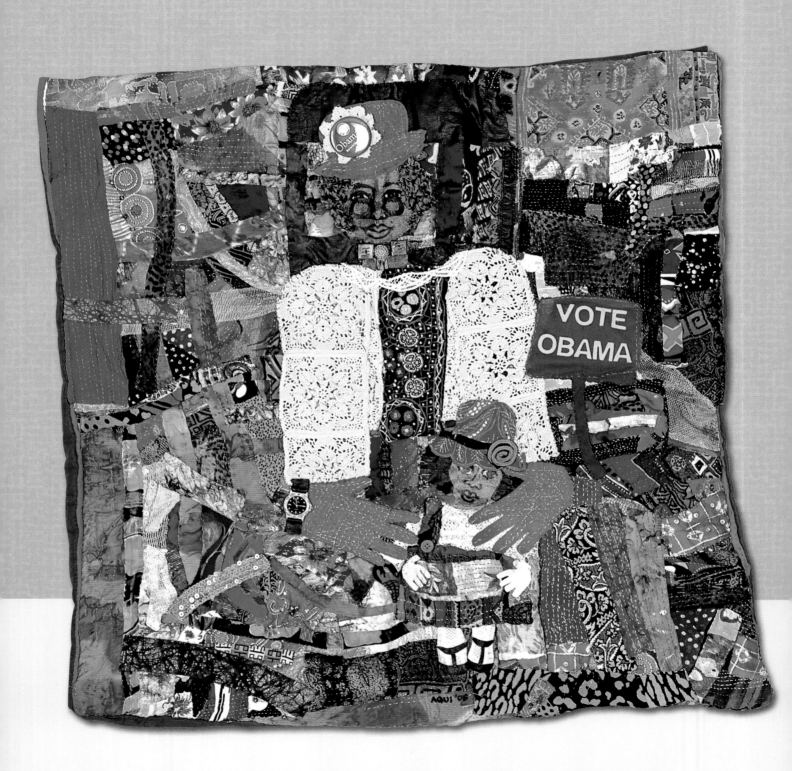

Gwendolyn Aqui
A New Day

My quilt is a portrait of Cora Ellie Mae Willis of Atlanta, Georgia, age eighty-three, and her beloved granddaughter Alexis Marie Willis, age three. Cora is sitting on her porch after voting for the first time. On the day she went to the polls, she stated, "I never thought I'd live to see a black man run for president of the United States. It is indeed a new day!"

A New Day

Gwendolyn Aqui l Washington, DC l 2008 l 36 x 36 inches (91 x 91 cm) l Cotton, beads, buttons, found objects l Hand appliquéd and hand stitched l *Photo by Chas. E. and Mary B. Martin*

Lauren Austin

Journeys Begin from Home

I went to Kenya during the summer of 2008 to teach art at an orphan care center in Kakamega in the Western Province. This area is close to the homestead of President Obama's father. My quilt contains images of some of the orphans and adults I grew to know and love and who taught me much more than I could teach them. Their dedication to each other and to the future of their country brought up memories of my own family and the African American struggle for human rights. Dignity exists in the struggle to excel in spite of hardships. Kenya and its people helped begin the journey for our president and, in a way, for me. I made the quilt to remember this inspiration. I celebrate our president and all of us.

Journeys Begin from Home

Lauren Austin ∣ Ningbo, Zhejiang, China ∣ 2008 ∣ 36 x 35 inches (91 x 89 cm) ∣ Silk, linen, and cotton, hand dyed by artist ∣ Painted, machine quilted, and hand embellished ∣ *Photo by Chas. E. and Mary B. Martin*

We Are a Nation

Alice Beasley | Oakland, California | 2009 | 36.5 x 42 inches (93 x 107 cm) | Cotton, silk |
Machine appliquéd, machine quilted, and hand-lettered border | *Photo by Don Tuttle*

Alice Beasley

We Are a Nation

Among the many reasons Obama has gained the respect of the world is his recognition that much more unites us than separates us; that we are not merely a group of factions to be pitted against each other. Consequently, I chose this quote from his inaugural address to frame his portrait:

"We are a nation of Christians and Muslims, Jews and Hindus, and nonbelievers. We are shaped by every language and culture, drawn from every end of this Earth. And because we have tasted the bitter swill of civil war and segregation and emerged from that dark chapter stronger and more united, we cannot help but believe that the old hatreds shall someday pass."

A Dream Realized

Carol Beck I Durham, North Carolina I 2008 I 34 x 34 inches (86 x 86 cm) I Commercial cottons I Hand and machine appliquéd; machine quilted I *Photo by Chas. E. and Mary B. Martin*

Carol Beck
A Dream Realized

This art quilt tribute represents a visual fabric journey of Barack Obama's life, culminating with a possible answer to poet Langston Hughes' plaintive question: "What happens to a dream deferred?" Hughes asks, "Does it dry up / Like a raisin in the sun?"

Barack Obama is a dreamer whose immediate family's dreams were deferred. This art quilt spotlights President Obama's love for basketball and four major life-stops during his formative years—Hawaii, New York, Massachusetts, and Illinois—as he prepared to follow his dream. The machine-appliquéd and hand-painted Obama portrait inside his campaign logo was constructed using over fifteen skin-tone fabrics to reflect our multiracial American family.

Young Barack recognized that if you use your time wisely, develop your skills, study, and diligently prepare for the future, a dream held in kindergarten can become a reality. When Barack Hussein Obama—our forty-fourth president—his wife, and two daughters stepped across the threshold of the White House on January 20, 2009, his childhood dream became a dream realized!

Sherry Boram
Dawn

The election of Barack Obama heralds the dawn of a better world.

Though the sun is depicted as rising to shine on the east coast of the United States, this dawn illuminates the entire planet, daily bringing us closer, with each revolution, to the world we want. President Obama is a courageous leader with qualities that most people of the world hold dear: honesty, integrity, wisdom, dignity, respect, and a willingness to work hard for all. He is the man for the times. Even as he focuses on solving monumental problems and promoting peace, I sense in him a capacity for joy that is never far from the surface. All this gives me hope.

Dawn

Sherry Boram l Pendleton, Indiana l 2009 l 37.5 x 36 inches (95 x 91 cm) l Commercial fabrics, decorative threads, yarns, metallic pigment, fixative, wool and cotton batting, fused raw-edge appliqué, and machine-couched yarns l Hand painted (Setacolor), stamped, and machine quilted l *Photo by Chas. E. and Mary B. Martin*

Edward Bostick

Thurgood Marshall, Supreme Court Justice

Fifteen years after the death of Justice Marshall, we, the citizens of the United States, shared in a common dream. We, as a strong, conscientious-minded nation of people, came together; voted and elected the first African American president, Barack Obama. This is a renaissance in history! Yes, pioneers like Thurgood Marshall made this significant endeavor possible. However, history has been germinating and ringing the bells of justice since the inception of time. As we continue marching into history—keeping hope alive—we will someday reach the mountaintop, and Dr. Martin Luther King Jr.'s speech will become a reality and all nations will be equal.

Thurgood Marshall, Supreme Court Justice

Edward M. Bostick I Brooklyn, New York I 2008 I 24 x 36 inches (61 x 91 cm) I Cotton, acrylic paint I Hand painted by Vinton Melbourne; quilted by Janice Jaminson I *Photo by Chas. E. and Mary B. Martin*

Diana Bracy
44ᵗʰ President and First Lady

My inspiration for creating this quilt was the feeling of love, contentment, and commitment captured in a photograph of the president and first lady. In deciding on the colors to use, I wanted the colors to be surprising and still capture their faces, which are filled with emotion.

When I create my art, I enlarge the photograph to select pixels. The pixels are used to collect the amount of detail that I would like to include in the final piece. This pattern is used as a guide, and batik fabric is selected in various colors and values. There are thousands of pieces of fabric, and each piece is fused to a backing. Some of the pieces are only one-quarter of an inch. Yes, only one-quarter of an inch!

As I was creating the art and seeing our first lady's smile emerge, I knew that I had selected just the right "unexpected" colors to portray the contentment on her face.

My excitement grew when I started on our president's silhouette and started filling in colors with fabric. He, too, came into view, and you can see his closed eye . . . smile.

Yes, his eye looks like it is smiling too.

Each evening, as I worked on the quilt, I would hang it on my design wall for inspection. As I walked around the quilt, I could see it in a 3-D image that my photo is unable to capture.

44th President and First Lady

Diana Bracy I Las Vegas, Nevada I 2009 I 25.5 x 20.5 inches (65 x 52 cm) I Cotton fabric, cotton thread, tricot, fusible web I Fused; machine quilted by Gwen Gwinner, Quilt Studio Ohio I *Photo by Chas. E. and Mary B. Martin*

Election Results

Laurie Brainerd I San Antonio, Texas I 2009 I 33 x 33 inches (84 x 84 cm) I Cotton fabric; silk, polyester, and cotton threads I Hand appliquéd, machine quilted I *Photo courtesy of the artist*

Laurie Brainerd
Election Results

Election Results was begun shortly after President Obama won the 2008 presidential election. I could feel the palpable hope that this country had after this monumental event. Apparently, I wasn't the only one, as "hope" became a mantra associated with President Obama.

I used the style of Robert Indiana's *Love*, which I knew growing up from the eight-cent stamp, to make my statement of hope. Love reflected that generation as hope reflects this one.

I call my style of quilting "quilting the hell out of it"—densely quilting almost the entire surface of each quilt. My favorite tool is my sewing machine's walking foot, because it allows me to create these wonderfully intricate quilted shapes that reveal other accidental shapes as the work is viewed from different angles.

For this quilt, I chose a traditional piecing pattern, the Lone Star. This represents our traditional American values: the norm, the status quo. Within this design, I quilted letters that spell out the word *change*, as that is what we, the American people, will have to do to meet the challenges that face us today. We are able to do this, as we now have hope.

Julius J. Bremer
My President

I made this quilt to celebrate the joy I felt in seeing the first African American president during my lifetime, at the age of fifty-five. It was always stated that *anyone* could become president, but in reality, I did not expect it so soon in this country.

The eyes reflect President Obama's view of the future for the United States, and his lips represent words of encouragement and that faith he has in the American people. His belief, that it is up to all of America to make us strong in the world's eyes, was the inspiration to make this quilt. I chose the blocks to represent the flags of the United States and Africa. The placards express some of the cheering cries of the people for change and cooperation during the election of 2008.

My President

Julius J. Bremer l Cleveland, Ohio l 2009 l 34 x 34 inches (86 x 86 cm) l Cotton fabric, acrylic paints, stenciling l Machine pieced and quilted l *Photo by Chas. E. and Mary B. Martin*

Carole Richburg Brown

Hear My Silent Song

Many of us have longed for a strong, responsible, highly qualified leader. We cried out for someone who could cross all lines of race, religion, and gender to serve our nation and our world. We sang our silent songs and prayed out loud and silently that one would come along who would fight the good fight for all. "We need justice," we sang, "and the world is going down the drain with unemployment, high crime, and low morals. Someone, please come and help us!" Barack Obama, you heard us. You heard our silent song, and you gave us hope. But more than hope, you said, "I can lead you and together we can change the world."

Hear My Silent Song

Carole Richburg Brown I Cleveland
Heights, Ohio I 2008 I 48 x 48 inches
(122 x 122 cm) I Cotton batik, dye
discharge I Stamped, fabric painted,
and free-motion quilted I *Photo by
Chas. E. and Mary B. Martin*

Wendell George Brown

Crossroads: Now Is the Time

In creating *Crossroads*, I thought about my great-great-great-grandmother Lilly Pruitt, a slave born in Georgia in 1805. I thought about my mother, Lovata Moss, and father, Augustus Brown, who grew up in and through segregation in the South. Finally, I thought about the journey of progress in the United States and how Barack Obama's win bridged a gap for cultural understanding and united people across racial boundaries.

Crossroads: Now Is the Time

Wendell George Brown I Columbia, South Carolina I 2009 I 32 x 32 inches (81 x 81 cm) I Commercial cottons, cotton canvas, acrylic paint I Hand painted and quilted I *Photo by Chas. E. and Mary B. Martin*

Bisa Butler
At Last

I voted for Barack Obama in my hometown elementary school gym, and I was one of those Americans who stood on the National Mall on a freezing January morning to see him inaugurated as the president of the United States. I didn't have one of the coveted tickets; I stood with the masses of humanity that converged on the Mall that morning.

Later that day, I watched Barack and Michelle dance to Beyoncé singing Etta James' song "At Last." My family and I watched with the rest of the nation to see what fabulous gown Michelle would have on. When the presidential couple stepped onto the stage and began their dance, it was a magical moment and we all crowded around the screen. There was a glow about the first couple, and as they swayed and twirled to the music, we all moved with them. I couldn't believe what I was seeing; I thought, "Could there be a more perfect moment?"

Never in our history as a nation, or more personally in my life, had I witnessed an event with such historic significance. It was the beauty of seeing a phenomenally happy and successful African American couple that brought tears to my eyes. Barack and Michelle, at that moment, represented a living fairytale prince and princess. "At Last" our time had come. I don't know what the slaves felt when they heard they were emancipated, but I think we all felt a tiny taste of that joy watching Barack and Michelle dance.

At Last

Bisa Butler I Bridgewater, New Jersey I 2009 I 46 x 40 inches (117 X 102 cm) I Cotton, chiffon, satin,
velvet, silk, and polyester I Machine appliquéd and quilted I *Photo by Chas. E. and Mary B. Martin*

One Vote Can Change the World

Bisa Butler I Bridgewater, New Jersey I 2008 I
27 x 38 inches (69 x 97 cm) I Hand-painted cotton,
commercial cotton, and denim I Machine appliquéd
and quilted I *Photo by Chas. E. and Mary B. Martin*

Bisa Butler

One Vote Can Change the World

One Vote Can Change the World is my homage to the amazing, beautiful, and powerful images I saw of Americans lining up to vote in this election. I had always heard about the struggles African Americans went through in order to gain the right to vote, but being of Generation X, I had never witnessed a movement before. During this election, I witnessed people of all ages, economic circumstances, and races lining up to ensure that Mr. Barack Obama would be our next president.

Denise M. Campbell

From Kenya to Kansas the World Rejoices

This quilt, depicting the world's reaction to Barack Obama's election, pays tribute to his heritage, his commitment to a sustainable White House, a green earth, and the celebration of hope. The quilt includes imagery from the upbringing that shaped his character. Diverse expressions of tears, dance, laughter, awe, and technology reflect the many ways in which this historic moment changed our global society forever.

From Kenya to Kansas the World Rejoices

Denise M. Campbell I Arroyo Grande, California I 2008 I
36 inches (91 cm) in diameter I Cotton I Hand and
machine appliquéd; machine quilted I *Photo by Chas. E.
and Mary B. Martin*

Cynthia Catlin
Blossom of Change

We now have a president who speaks for the voiceless and inspires us all to achieve our greatest potential. His promise of change brings hope and gives us the strength to endure. I am hopeful our journey will enlighten us as we realize a greater sense of community. The promise will blossom as we continue the journey and realize the dream that will transform our lives and our nation forever.

Blossom of Change

Cynthia Catlin I San Pedro, California I 2009 I 48 x 39 inches (122 x 99 cm) I Cotton I Machine appliquéd and quilted I *Photo by Chas. E. and Mary B. Martin*

The promise of CHANGE

Betty Coburn

Obama Drafted for the NBA

"May you live in interesting times" means that heroes or leaders emerge from turbulent times. The years 2000 to 2008 have presented every imaginable kind of turbulent time in our country and the world. I was appalled by what passed for leadership during that time.

I am happy our new president displays thoughtful attention to the unique and competing challenges in our country and the world. I am grateful our new president listens to what others have to say and has surrounded himself with smart, deep-thinking people of action. I am pleased our new president is willing to be honest with us about the difficult road ahead. I am relieved our new president understands how real life works for real citizens and families. And, most of all, I am delighted our new president has a sense of humor about himself and loves to play basketball.

My husband believes that the most important things in life can be learned on a basketball court. In basketball one must pay attention to what nine other people are doing and coordinate with four of them—while on the move. One must be quick thinking, flexible on short notice, and agile. One must have the stamina to finish the game, the maturity to accept reality, and the vision to work toward the best outcome.

Barack Obama first intrigued me with his global perspective, concern for real people, and thoughtful, intelligent manner of speaking and writing. I love his level-headed patience in dealing with issues and personalities.

Obama Drafted for the NBA is my tribute to the difficult task that our new president faces. May he approach leadership as a good "streetballer" and perform a National Balancing Act.

Obama Drafted for the NBA

Betty Colburn I Portland, Oregon I 2008 I 34 x 28 inches (86 x 71 cm) I Commercial cottons, cotton batting I Machined pieced and quilted; photo printed on cotton with Durabrite ink I *Photo by Chas. E. and Mary B. Martin*

Marion Coleman

Speaking of Women

***Speaking of Women* is a mixed-media fiber collage** that showcases painted and stitched images of several women in the Obama family. Thread-written words fill the background with positive traits associated with the women, combined with the uneven edge. My quilt symbolizes the patchwork of women's lives, including growth and change.

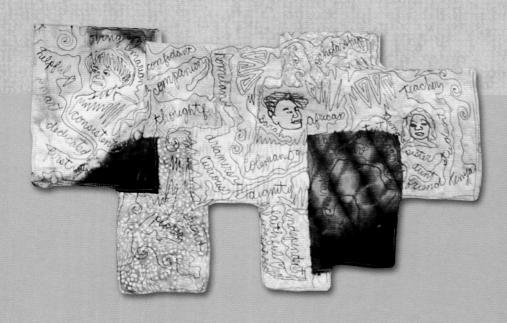

Speaking of Women

Marion Coleman I Castro Valley, California I 2009 I 39 x 34.5 inches (99 x 88 cm) I Oil pastels, cotton, African batik, thread, batting I Painted and thread drawn, thread written, raw-edge pieced, and machine quilted I *Photo by Chas. E. and Mary B. Martin*

Marion Coleman
Winds for Change

Winds for Change presents the journey to the American presidency by Barack Obama. The background documents African Americans who have served in the Senate and House of Representatives from Reconstruction to the present. Recognized and lesser-known African Americans who have run for president of the United States are also presented as a backdrop to the election process. With red state/blue state colors surrounding civil rights stamps, election buttons, election ballots, and news clips, the piece explores the path that led to this historic election.

Winds for Change

Marion Coleman I Castro Valley, California I 2009 I 32.5 x 33.5 inches (83 x 85 cm) I Cotton, silk, postage stamps, campaign buttons, thread I Digitally printed, fused, and machine quilted I *Photo by Chas. E. and Mary B. Martin*

Light at the End of the Tunnel

Connie Condrell I Washington, D.C. I 2008 I 42 x 60 inches (107 x 152 cm) I
Commercial cottons, yarns I Printed, batiked, machine pieced, and hand
quilted I *Collection of Elise Riley and John Simpson* I *Photo by Mary Stanley*

Connie Condrell

Light at the End of the Tunnel

I often listen to the radio as I work at my design wall. As I moved the small individual fabric squares around on this piece, I listened to the candidates campaigning for the U.S. presidency.

Barack Obama impressed me when he gave the keynote address at the Democratic National Convention in 2004. I sensed then that he might run for president himself one day. "Now there's a man I could vote for," I thought. Not in my wildest dreams did I ever imagine it would happen so fast.

I marveled at his intelligence and understanding of what was going on in our country and how we were perceived around the world. I listened carefully to his ideas on how we might begin to change the way things are done by our government in order to better serve all Americans. I heard his desire to have the United States partner with other countries to solve our global problems instead of making unilateral decisions because we're a powerful force to be feared. My hope grew as I listened to him describe his dream for our future.

I found my quilt taking on the form of a dark, tunnel-like spiral that ends in a burst of light. This light represents a chance, finally, for our government to make some of the changes we need so badly. I was thrilled when Barack Obama was elected, and I look forward to his leading us in doing the hard but necessary work that will put our country on the right track.

Donnette A. Cooper

America at the Crossroads

I was inspired to create this quilt, *America at the Crossroads*, during the course of the 2008 presidential campaign. The purportedly "improbable" candidacy of Barack Hussein Obama demanded intro/retrospection about America's perennial challenge to reconcile the competing imperatives of race, gender, religion, class, nationality, and sexual identity as we struggle to realize the vision of "a more perfect union."

As I engaged in debating, donating, campaigning, and, finally, protecting the vote on Election Day, it became apparent to me that America was at a crucial crossroads and we needed a wise and audacious interpreter/mediator to negotiate the crossing. As a Jamaican American immigrant, Barack Obama's narrative resonated with me. Obama, who is black and white, insider and outsider, native and other, acknowledged our stories, explained our fears, and inspired us to make a united leap of faith into a future where we become the change we have been waiting for.

The Ghanaian *adinkrahene* symbol, anchoring the corners of the inner border of the quilt, denotes greatness, charisma, and leadership. The central *adinkra* symbol of the intertwined crocodiles, *funtunfunefu-denkyemfunefu*, signifies unity in diversity. The bicolored representation of the same symbol at the outer border of the quilt invokes the spirit of the Yoruba orisha Esu-Elegbara—mediator, joiner of opposites, opener of gates, and guardian of the crossroads.

With mathematical precision, this quilt delineates the intersecting social and political movements that have enabled the election of Barack Obama as our forty-fourth president. *America at the Crossroads* emblematizes the possibility of regeneration of the United States in the twenty-first century.

America at the Crossroads

Donnette A. Cooper I Hyattesville, Maryland I 2008 I 92 x 92 inches (234 x 234 cm) I Cotton and cowrie shells I Hand and machine appliquéd, machine pieced, machine quilted by Julia Graves I *Photo by Kim Johnson*

Carolyn Crump
From Vision to Victory

Celebrating the inauguration of the forty-fourth president of the United States, my quilt captures the momentum of generations. From repression, Americans have chiseled proud resistance; from struggle, leadership; from sacrifice, hope for all to come. With a single purpose, collectively these Americans built the bedrock on which a nation's promise now is realized. Every stitch traces that sweep of history, and I celebrate with the nation and the world the brilliance of a new day.

From Vision to Victory

Carolyn Crump I Houston, Texas I 2008 I 36 x 31.5 inches (91 x 80 cm) I Cotton I Machine appliquéd; hand and thread painted I *Collection of Dr. Carolyn L. Mazloomi* I *Photo by Chas. E. and Mary B. Martin*

Carolyn Crump
Michelle

The motivation to quilt this piece came from seeing the strength and boldness in our first lady's cheeks, the caring in her eyes, and the security of her smile. I can visualize little girls of all backgrounds looking up at this quilt and thinking, "When I grow up, I want to be just like Michelle Obama." Even as someone my age, I felt very honored and blessed for the opportunity to create the piece.

Michelle

Carolyn Crump I Houston, Texas I 2008 I 14 x 18 inches (36 x 46 cm) I Cotton, photo transfer I Free-motion quilted I *Photo courtesy of the artist*

Warrior of Light Shield for Obama

Adriene Cruz I Portland, Oregon I 2008 I
36 x 37 inches (91 x 94 cm) I Embellished fabric,
cowrie shells, mirrors, lemon verbena, assorted
talismans, beetle wings, and prayers I Pieced and
hand stitched I *Photo by Art Alexander*

Adriene Cruz

Warrior of Light Shield for Obama

Warrior of Light Shield for Obama **is a quilted talisman** honoring our forty-fourth president, Barack Hussein Obama, whose radiant light shines well beyond the borders of the United States.

Drawing on the positive energy of the millions who wish Barack Obama and his family well, I imagined the healing light of God composed of love, power, and wisdom, and I created an embellished shield offering prayers and blessings for protection and peace.

This talisman is a compilation of many good luck charms and blessings, including cowrie shells, *adinkra* symbols, the eye of Shiva, mirrors, leaves of lemon verbena, iridescent beetle wings, and the Robe of Light prayer.

It is hoped that the positive vibrations embedded in this quilted talisman are as radiant and powerful as the love between Michelle and Barack Obama.

Freedom's Box

Eileen Doughty | Vienna, Virginia | 2009 | 33 x 34 inches (84 x 86 cm) | Cottons, glitter paint, organza, inks | Machined pieced, appliquéd, fused, and quilted | *Photo by artist*

Eileen Doughty
Freedom's Box

George W. Bush often spoke of freedom and bringing democracy to other countries. In doing so, he opened a Pandora's box, releasing troubles into the world. But, as in the original myth, hope remains. Here, the statue of Freedom has descended from the top of the Capitol dome and opens the box. Hope—Obama's theme—is symbolized by the golden brown bird with the golden beak. As with all my political quilts, my greyhound—my symbol of Everyman—is included in the scene. The box design and Freedom's seated position are based on ancient Greek artwork. I added the Greek word for "free."

61

Jacqueline Dukes
Oahu, Ohana, Obama

Once I read Mr. Obama's autobiography, I knew he was destined for greater heights than ever imagined. I thought, "What a smart man to admit to teenage indiscretions and family idiosyncrasies, thus preventing a spoiler from later surfacing to derail his plans." I observed and enjoyed.

Mr. Obama presents such a cool exterior, but when he speaks, there is such passion. I chose colors to celebrate the man and his childhood home. Water and fire represent his demeanor, words honor the orator, and fish connect to his father's people and represent brain food. Hawaiian colors were used for the backing in support of that unique multicultural environment, which nurtured this gift to the world. Needing to do something just for him, I discharge dyed the name *Obama* on the fabric so nobody else would have the same material.

There is such depth to Mr. Obama that I think of the ocean surrounding Oahu and the endless night skies. I'm reminded of the volcanoes that formed the islands as a symbol of his presence during the campaign. Those who underestimated his power were devastated as he flowed smoothly past them. As I hand quilted each section, additional descriptions of President Obama came to mind and I wrote them on the quilt. To complete the quilt, I added beads with words written on them, and there are the fish to represent the family and the ancestors. My heart filled with joy as I formed each stitch!

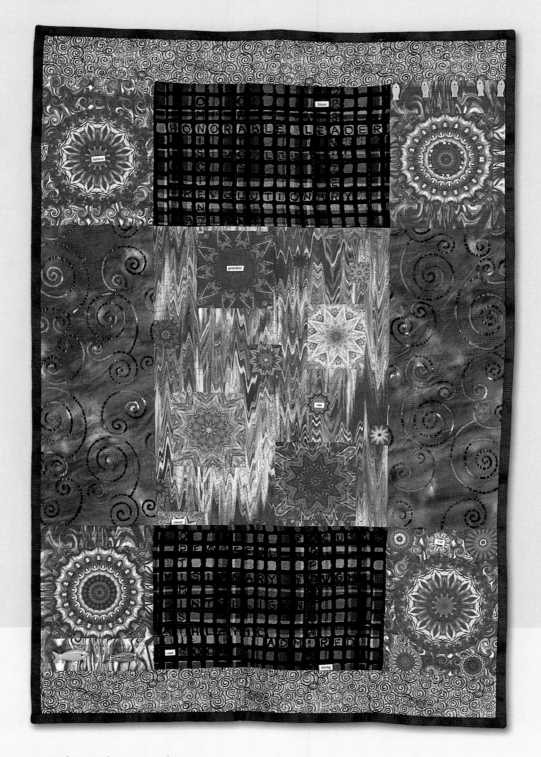

Oahu, Ohana, Obama

Jacqueline Dukes I Shaker Heights, Ohio I 2009 I 54 x 34 inches (137 x 86 cm) I Computer-generated cotton, variegated rayon threads I Hand quilted and pieced, painted, discharge dyed, and stamped I *Photo by Chas. E. and Mary B. Martin*

Change Has Come

Ife Felix | New York, New York | 2009 | 35 x 28 inches (89 x 71 cm) | African and domestic cotton | Machine pieced and hand quilted | *Photo by Alphonso Ferris*

Ife Felix
Change Has Come

I was inspired to make *Change Has Come* the first time I saw Barack Obama, an African American man seriously running for president of the United States. Hearing Mr. Obama speak, I began to imagine the possibilities of change in America.

Not sure where I would go with it, I began with the basic red, white, and blue fabric and waited for inspiration. The untitled quilt, a work in progress, remained in my studio as I watched the campaign closely. I felt for the first time I was being represented. I saw Obama's vision for America and wanted to be a part of it in honor of all those who gave their lives for this change. Never owning a flag, I decided to redesign it to celebrate the hope I felt for me and my fellow Americans.

The election of Barack Obama as the forty-fourth president of the United States was one of the most exciting moments in American history. I finished the quilt after hearing his brilliant inaugural speech. I realized that a part of the journey taken by Americans so many years ago had been reached. We are a better country and people because "Change Has Come."

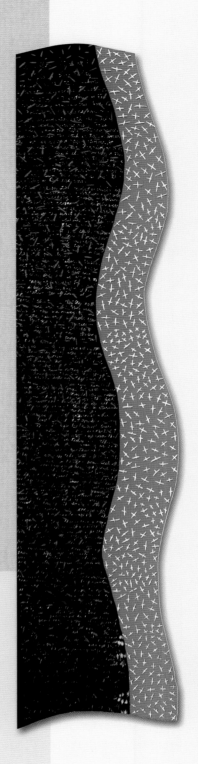

Deborah Fell

And Then There Was Hope

President Obama came to the University of Illinois in 2004 while running for the U.S. Senate. Hearing him speak for the first time, I felt hope unlike anything I have ever experienced before in our national arena. The picture I took hung on my studio inspiration wall for a number of years before Mr. Obama was elected our president.

Starting in September 2008, several months before the election, I knew only a few things about the ultimate visual image I was trying to portray. The face of Obama needed to became all colors of the world, since he has a global connection to so many. The word *hope*, embedded into the piecing, serves as one of the fundamental design images. Mr. Obama gave the state of Illinois hope during his Senate election and again in the presidential campaign. His words during the year before the election set our country on fire with a lucidity we desperately needed. The words, too, had to be a central design figure.

Besides being a studio artist, I am also a veteran public high school teacher with over thirty years teaching experience. Like a patchwork quilt, my dual lives are interwoven. I brainstormed with ninth- and tenth-grade students, and my question to them was, "What words come to mind when you think of the election?" The words the students generated were indicative of the awareness they had of the election and its importance. Twenty-five of the words were from an autistic student.

And then there was hope . . .

And Then There Was Hope

Deborah Fell I Urbana, Illinois I 2009 I 39 x 34 inches (99 x 86 cm) I Cotton, fiber-reactive dyes, large-scale digital printing, digital imaging software I Pieced, appliquéd, fused, machine quilted I *Photo by Chas. E. and Mary B. Martin*

Fiber Artists for Obama

Yes! We Can

In starting the Fiber Artists for Obama group on the official Obama website, founder Lisa Shepard Stewart simply saw it as a fun way of merging two of her passions: fiber arts and the presidential candidacy of Barack Obama. "The Obama website made it so easy to start a group (going back to its theme of inclusion and accessibility!), and so it began. I felt sure there would be many others who shared these interests . . . and I knew that whatever did emerge would be interesting."

After endless e-mails regarding the parameters of the quilt, we decided that each 12-inch block should incorporate a shade of blue-purple to help unify the blocks when joined together. Each block was to also feature a buzzword from the campaign, such as *change*, *hope*, and even *fist bump*.

In the end, fifteen blocks were submitted by the deadline; these were joined and surrounded by pieced borders. It was an honor to have it hang at Quilt Festival in Houston (2008), and after inclusion in various shows and exhibits, we plan to present it to the first family. The quilt is now touring museums around the country in the Journey of Hope in America exhibition sponsored by the National Afro-American Museum and Cultural Center of Wilberforce, Ohio.

The following artists contributed quilt blocks:

Diana Bracy (Las Vegas, Nevada)

Carolyn Bunkley (Detroit, Michigan)

Gerrie Congdon (Portland, Oregon)

Cherryl Floyd-Miller (Charleston, South Carolina)

Lynette S. Jackson (Marietta, Georgia)

Erma Johnson (Chicago, Illinois)

Caron Lage (St. Cloud, Minnesota)

Monna Morton (Philadelphia, Pennsylvania)

Sharon Rogers (Decatur, Georgia)

Lisa Shepard Stewart (Rahway, New Jersey)

Susan Shie (Wooster, Ohio)

Jacqueline Stafford (Suitland, Maryland)

Rita Strickland (New York, New York)

The blocks were sashed by Mary Bowman and her daughter Stephanie Scott (Riverside, California). The borders, quilting, and binding were done by Maria C. Shell (Anchorage, Alaska).

Yes! We Can

Fiber Artists for Obama l 2008 l 82 x 59 inches (208 x 150 cm) l Traditional and nontraditional patchwork and photo transfer l *Photo by Chas. E. and Mary B. Martin*

Michelle D. Flamer

Next

Seven years after _Brown v. Board of Education,_ my parents had the courage to place their five-year-old black daughter on public transportation so I could receive a better public school education out of our district. My parents were threatened with legal action, but they prevailed in keeping me in the then all-white school. When school integration began in earnest a few years later, Philadelphia school officials hastily added "Negro History" to the curriculum. I can remember the "textbook," which consisted of spiral-bound photocopies of stories of blacks who had contributed to this country. Alongside Charles Drew and George Washington Carver were pages devoted to Diahann Carroll and Louis Armstrong. Even at that young age, I was disappointed by the book's presentation and content. The "real" history book, which was hardbound, taught of presidents and serious topics of war and freedom. I dreamed for a day when the substantive achievements of African Americans would be taught and celebrated. I was actually hopeful enough as a child to dream of a black president.

The intervening years, which saw the assassinations of Martin Luther King Jr. and John F. Kennedy, did little to encourage my dream. Yet like many, I was captivated by Barack Obama's speech at the 2004 Democratic National Convention. I was tired of the red state/blue state polarization in our country and wildly applauded his call for a "United" States of America. When I had the opportunity to meet him a few months later, during his appearance in Philadelphia to support John Kerry's candidacy, I knew firsthand that this man could be my president someday. Beyond his intellect and oratory skills, I caught a brief glimpse of his compassion, patience, and confidence.

My quilts are my historical documentation of this moment in time.

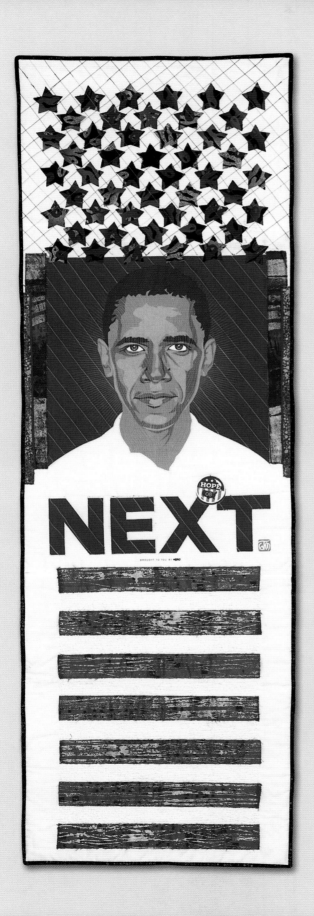

Next

Michelle D. Flamer I Philadelphia,
Pennsylvania I 2008 I 60 x 24 inches
(152 x 61 cm) I Cotton and acrylic
paint I Hand painted in collaboration
with Ray Noland and machine
quilted I *Photo by Chas. E. and
Mary B. Martin*

The Journey: We Are the Ones We Have Been Waiting For

L'Merchie Frazier I Dorchester, Massachusetts I 2008 I 36 inches (91 cm) in diameter I Cotton, silk, paper I Photo transfer on silk and hand stitched I *Photo by Chas. E. and Mary B. Martin*

L'Merchie Frazier

The Journey: We Are the Ones We Have Been Waiting For

November 4, 2008, marked the critical, full-circle milestone in a journey begun with the story of human rights, civil rights, and voting in America. That day, throngs of people were welcomed, were united, and shared the gift of time and change, electing the first black president of the United States. He stands on the shoulders of a long line of history that fashioned this moment and the long lines of people who cast their ballots to make manifest a national and global victory. This quilt celebrates the vote cast by my ninety-three-year-old mother, 143 years of voting suffrage, and the making of the forty-fourth president of the United States, Barack Obama.

Quilt title excerpted from Barack Obama's Super Tuesday speech, delivered February 19, 2008, Chicago, Illinois.

Yes We Can… and in My Lifetime

Marjorie Diggs Freeman I Durham, North Carolina I 2008 I 33 x 33.5 (84 x 85 cm) I Cotton fabrics, cotton batting I Hand pieced and appliquéd; hand quilted I *Photo by Chas. E. and Mary B. Martin*

Marjorie Diggs Freeman
Yes We Can . . . and in My Lifetime

The time is now to bring about real change to the country we love.

Prior to the 2008 election, the last time I was this excited about a presidential election was when I voted in my first one for John F. Kennedy! Initially, given my country's history, I never believed that an African American could be elected president of the United States in my lifetime. But that all changed in the twenty-first century when Barack Obama delivered the keynote address, "The Audacity of Hope," at the 2004 Democratic National Convention. His spirit, intelligence, charisma, and delivery told me then that he was not only special but a unique individual that America would hear from again and again in the future. Fate had placed him front and center for all America to hear and see . . . and to remember.

I would not consider myself politically active, but I joined the Obama campaign because as a black American, I was going to do my best to get Barack Obama elected! The main fabrics for this quilt were bought during the primaries because Obama was going to be the subject of a quilt, win or lose, because he was making American history! During the week of the 2008 Democratic National Convention, when Barack Obama was nominated as the Democrats' official candidate for president of the United States, I was so inspired that I created this design in prayerful hope of his election. I chose to capture that historical moment using a favorite technique, hand appliqué, in fabrics representative of the American flag, as he would be the president of all the people. I made a larger version of this quilt initially (with more photo transfers) for my local guild's quilt show to remind people to vote for hope and Barack Obama!

This quilt, completed for the exhibit Quilts for Obama: An Exhibit Celebrating the Inauguration of Our 44th President, which opened in Washington, DC, in January 2009, is made completely by hand. President Obama inspired a nation to have the audacity to HOPE again and therefore to change. I never dreamed that I would live to see an African American president leading the United States of America, therefore the title: Yes We Can . . . and in My Lifetime.

Debra Gabel

It's a New Day!

It's a New Day! was started in 2008 when I was learning about Barack Obama and the obvious impact he was going to have on the world. Every time I heard him speak, I was inspired and I thought, "This is what this world needs right now." The day after he was elected, I received a phone call from a friend, who knows my work and happens to be a female African American physician, who wanted to commission me to design and make a quilt honoring Obama. After that phone call, the quilt was hers. She wanted something very important to commemorate this historic event that would become a family heirloom.

The quilt pictures President Obama looking bravely to the future. The backdrop is the U.S. flag, which has been pieced with hundreds of scraps representing the diverse cultures of America. The dove, which is in the upper left corner, is the pure symbol for hope that Obama emits with his mere presence. The three stars that circle his head represent the Father, Son, and Holy Ghost, who I pray helps guide him in leading our nation out of the crisis we face today. The quilt is turned appliqué of 100 percent cottons. It was designed, constructed, and quilted by me on a home sewing machine. There is a "d.g." watermark logo embroidered on the bottom right, which is in all my art quilts. You will notice the red bands on three sides of the quilt edge. This is my unique way of dating the quilt. The top edge has one red stripe sewn into the border; that represents the first month of the year—January. The left top edge has two red bars, which stand for the twenty-first century, and the bottom right has nine bands, which represent the year. Hence the quilt was made in January 2009.

I am quite proud of this quilt, as I am proud to be an American living in this great country.

It's a New Day!

Debra Gabel I Clarksville, Maryland I 2009 I 50 x 54 inches (127 x 137 cm) I Cotton fabric, fabric paint, embellishments I Pieced, turned-edge appliqué, painted I *Collection of Nadu Tauki* I *Photo by artist*

Sandra German

Reflecting on Our Victory

Reflecting on Our Victory is a rendering of a magnificent tree selected to symbolize the magnitude and impact of the campaign and election of President Barack Hussein Obama. Like this tree, the first African American U.S. president is already casting a giant shadow all around the world. Significantly, it is his connection to us that I emphasize here. We are his base, his anchor. We are the soil itself. We are tied to him in our roots, and we have enriched the earth with the blood and bones and spirits of our ancestors.

In *Reflecting on Our Victory*, I present the "Obama tree"; anchored in the knowledge of the ages, watched over by a sky that has seen a thousand pyramids, situated in uncertain times, and reflecting fragments of our own resurrected pride. His campaign was unprecedented—buoyed by an army of first-timers, young and old, and characterized by everything from true believers to the once jaded turned guardedly optimistic. Many openly confessed that, for the first time, they had found new resonance and meaning in what had formerly been only hollow words and empty symbols. For them, because of Obama's election, America itself had changed. This was for them a time of metamorphosis.

We talk about and look forward to change with Obama. Notice that I have placed a bird high in the tree. It represents a *sankofa* bird. In African folklore, the *sankofa* bird is an enduring symbol of caution. Wherever seen, it reminds us to remember the lessons of the past before we step blindly into the future. This coincides with the time-proven warning that those who don't learn the lessons of the past are doomed to repeat them. The year of Obama's victory was also a year that saw hate crimes in a schoolyard in Jena, Louisiana, and bombs in Gaza, Palestine. As we look forward, we must be vigilant and help ensure that any "change" instituted by the Obama presidency is change that is substantive, meaningful, and mindful of the past, present, and future. It is change that must reflect us.

Reflecting on Our Victory

Sandra K. German I Monroeville, Pennsylvania I 2009 I 80 x 85 inches (203 x 216 cm) I
Men's shirting, various cottons, oil and acrylic paint, *shisha* mirrors, findings, and
embellishments I Patchwork, appliquéd, hand painted, machine embroidered, *broderie
perse*, and machine quilted I *Photo by Chas. E. and Mary B. Martin*

You Dig?

Martha Gilbert I Ellicott City, Maryland I 2009 I 42 x 40 inches (107 x 102 cm) I
Commercial and artist-dyed/painted cottons, synthetic yarns, and rayon thread
I Pieced, appliquéd, painted, stenciled I *Photo by Paul Gilbert*

Martha Gilbert
You Dig?

The day after Barack Obama was elected president of the United States, my son's blog had this quote as its headline: "They still call it the White House, but that's a temporary condition, you dig?" I knew immediately that it would be the focus of a piece on the Obama election.

You Dig? is the latest in a series of Spokeswomen quilts that I have been making since 2000. They are not self-portraits, other than to say things that I have been thinking. They can be loud, humorous, confident, outspoken, and in this case triumphant. The multihued, postracial woman in *You Dig?* is announcing a sea of change in American history.

Valerie Goodwin
African Burial Ground

For me, maps are intriguing as an art form and as a vehicle for artistic expression.
They are personal explorations of map language and imagined landscapes. Most of my pieces
are not consciously based on a specific place. However, the story of the African Burial Ground,
a real place, served as the inspiration for this particular work. The previously forgotten and
hidden life of African slaves living on this particular site spoke to me as a vehicle for artistic
examination. Much of what I chose to include in this quilt was learned from a book entitled
Breaking Ground, Breaking Silence, written by Joyce Hansen.

The burial ground for African slaves was discovered in 1991 during the excavation for the
Foley Square Federal Building in lower Manhattan. During construction, workers uncovered
the biggest colonial cemetery for slaves and free Africans in our nation. Reportedly, more than
twenty thousand Africans living in the Dutch colony of New York were part of this moving
and dramatic discovery.

On the left side of this quilt is a map of the slave farmlands, the cemetery, and Dutch
settlement during 1755. It is said that the slaves were given these lands to be a buffer zone
between the colonists and the hostile Indians to the north. The right side of this quilt is a map
of lower Manhattan as it exists today. The quilt is anchored on the bottom with an imaginary
scene of the burial site.

The *adinkra* symbol of Ghana, *sankofa* means "go back and fetch it," and it was found on
some of the slave artifacts. The goal of this piece was to celebrate our remarkable journey in
this country—especially in light of the recent election of our nation's first African American
president. For me, it was important that this subject matter inform my art in order to map the
memories and experiences of our history as slaves.

African Burial Ground

Valerie S. Goodwin I Tallahassee, Florida I 2009 I 32 x 44 inches (81 x 112 cm) I Cotton, sheers, paints, digitally printed fabric, thread I Pieced, fused, raw-edge machine appliquéd, machine and hand quilted I *Photo by Richard Brunck*

Myrah Green
Children Dancin' at the Tree of Life

Children Dancin' at the Tree of Life depicts children in various **American cultures** wearing red, white, and blue clothing celebrating at a tree of life. The Egyptian ankh symbol and Ghana's *gye nyame* symbol are placed in the tree bark, representing long life, protection, infinite wisdom, and omnipotent spirit for our forty-fourth president. This quilt is a part of my Dancing at the Tree of Life quilt series. Over the years, the tree has been a monumental place where those of African descent have congregated for spiritual gatherings, weddings, births, special announcements, and to salute the deceased.

Children Dancin' at the Tree of Life

Myrah Green I Brooklyn, New York I 2008 I 31 x 32 inches (79 x 81 cm) I Cotton, cowrie shells I Machine pieced and appliquéd; free-motion quilted I *Photo by Chas. E. and Mary B. Martin*

Sandra Hankins
Everybody's All American

I was inspired to do this quilt because I've been a huge admirer of President Obama since 2004, when he was the junior senator of Illinois. I remember the Democratic Convention, where he made a groundbreaking keynote speech. I remember vividly that at one point in his address, he spoke of one America. "There's not a liberal America and a conservative America; there's the United States of America. There's not a black America and white America and Latino America and Asian America; there's the United States of America." I was so blown away by his words, both then and still now. We're so blessed to have Barack Obama as our country's leader.

Everybody's All American

Sandra Hankins I Murrieta, California I 2009 I 38 x 24 inches (97 x 61 cm)
I Tsukineko inks, buttons, crystals, and ribbons I Thread painted and hand
painted I *Collection of Norm and Della Mcloyn* I *Photo by Chas. E. and
Mary B. Martin*

Carole Harris

O + C = 44

Inspired by the events surrounding the recent sea change election of our forty-fourth president, I endeavored to commemorate the event with a work that utilized the text, colors, and symbols of the 2008 campaign. I wanted to comment in a way that was stylistically recognizable as my own but that was also specific to the event. I chose to employ my usual strip piecing, using text conveying slogans and messages of change and hope, along with the date and the colors of the Obama campaign—red, white, blue, and sky blue—which vary greatly from my normal palette. Graphically, the image on the right is a stylized "44," and the shape of the piece is horizontal, like a flag. The thirteen red and white stripes in the upper left-hand corner symbolize the thirteen colonies, which were the beginning of these United States, and give a nod to how far we have come as a nation. The quilting in the large navy blue area is a version of the circular Obama logo with the road going over the horizon.

This quilt was a challenge, not only because of the stylistic and process change it presented but also because it is impossible to crystallize, in one small work, the magnitude and range of emotions that this event represents. I suspect there will be more to come.

O + C = 44

Carole Harris I Detroit, Michigan I 2009 I
60.5 x 38.5 inches (154 x 98 cm) I Commercial
cottons I Machine pieced by Laura Rodin I
Photo by Chas. E. and Mary B. Martin

Restoration

Peggie Hartwell I Summerville, South Carolina I 2008 I 36 x 34 inches (91 x 86 cm) I Cotton, fabric ink I Machine appliquéd and quilted I *Photo by Chas. E. and Mary B. Martin*

Peggie Hartwell

Restoration

Our Beloved Soldiers of the Cause

(those who have sojourned on), you would be so proud. He has arrived: tall, strong, and determined to restore and reclaim our dignity. Out of Africa his father hailed.

Our Beloved Soldiers of the Cause (those who are still with us), thank you so much for your initial steps. Out of a sense of justice, you called forth your courage and paved the way. We are forever grateful to you all. It was the "single" dream of a multitude that brought this day into being. Now it has come to pass. So let us celebrate, let us "lift our voices and sing." For in our lifetime, we have thought the unthinkable—we have made possible an impossible dream: the first African American to become president of the United States: Barack Obama.

In my tribute quilt, President Obama "runs stairs" up to the White House. There are names inscribed on some of the steps over which he passes, and these names are an integral part of my design. These are the names of key people who have been part of the civil rights movement—who laid down their spirits, minds, and sometimes even their bodies so that this great day might come. Of course, there were countless others, too, and I do not forget them. These names are symbols of them all.

Thurgood Marshall First African American to serve as a justice on the U.S. Supreme Court

Linda Brown Little girl who fought the Board of Education of Topeka, Kansas, in the U.S. Supreme Court and who thereby helped all American children receive a better education

Sojourner Truth Former slave who preached against slavery

Homer Plessy Like Rosa Parks, he was arrested for being in the "wrong" section of a train. He fought against discrimination in the landmark U.S. Supreme Court case of *Plessy v. Ferguson.*

Mary McLeod Bethune Created schools for black students; worked with several U.S. presidents to make sure that all American children received good educations

Rosa Parks Considered the mother of the civil rights movement; worked with civil rights organization to start the Montgomery Bus Boycott

Dr. Martin Luther King Jr. Clergyman, activist, 1964 Nobel Peace Prize winner

Frederick Douglass Formerly enslaved; poet and abolitionist

Harriet Tubman Formerly enslaved; worked to free other slaves

Medgar Evers Fighter for the rights of black students

Rudy Bridges Helped end segregation in American schools; the first black student in her elementary school

Malcolm X Civil rights activist; worked to end segregation

91

·EVEN THOUGH WE FACE THE DIFFICULTIES
OF TODAY AND TOMORROW, I STILL HAVE A
DREAM. IT IS A DREAM DEEPLY ROOTED IN THE
AMERICAN DREAM·
Dr. Martin Luther King

American Dream

Sylvia Hernandez | Brooklyn, New York | 2009 | 58 x 58 inches (147 x 147 cm) | Cotton fabric, appliqué | Hand embroidered, machine pieced and quilted | *Photo by Deneka Peniston*

Sylvia Hernandez
American Dream

This quilt was started during the presidential campaign.
I wanted some way of expressing what so many were feeling. I started
with the Underground Railroad pattern from the book by Eleanor Burns
and Sue Bouchard. The text came from the "I Have a Dream" speech by
Dr. Martin Luther King Jr. I wanted to include an image of President Obama
and to show him emerging from this history. I have had such a great reaction
to this quilt—from my family, my pastor and other people from my church
(Epiphany Church), members of the Quilters' Guild of Brooklyn, and other
artists—that I would be so happy for others to see it as well. I think President
Obama gives us all hope for a better future and inspires us to dream big.

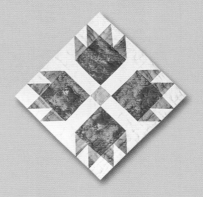

Sylvia Hernandez
Obama Hawaiian Style

This quilt was inspired by Hawaiian quilts, which I thought appropriate since the president is from Hawaii. The patterns on the four corners are the word *hope* cut out like a snowflake pattern, and the blue on the top center is the word *change*. The hibiscus on the left is the state flower of Hawaii; the other flower is the American beauty rose, which is the official flower of Washington DC. The flag is from Inauguration Day, and the center is from a T-shirt I purchased in Washington DC.

Obama Hawaiian Style

Sylvia Hernandez I Brooklyn, New York I 2009 I 59 x 59 inches (150 x 150 cm) I Cotton fabric, appliqué I Machine pieced and quilted I *Photo by Deneka Peniston*

YES WE DID
UNITED IN PROGRESS TOWARD A MORE PERFECT UNION
PEOPLE
POWERED
NOVEMBER 4TH 2008
44th President
Barack Obama
Inauguration Day Flag
1-20-09

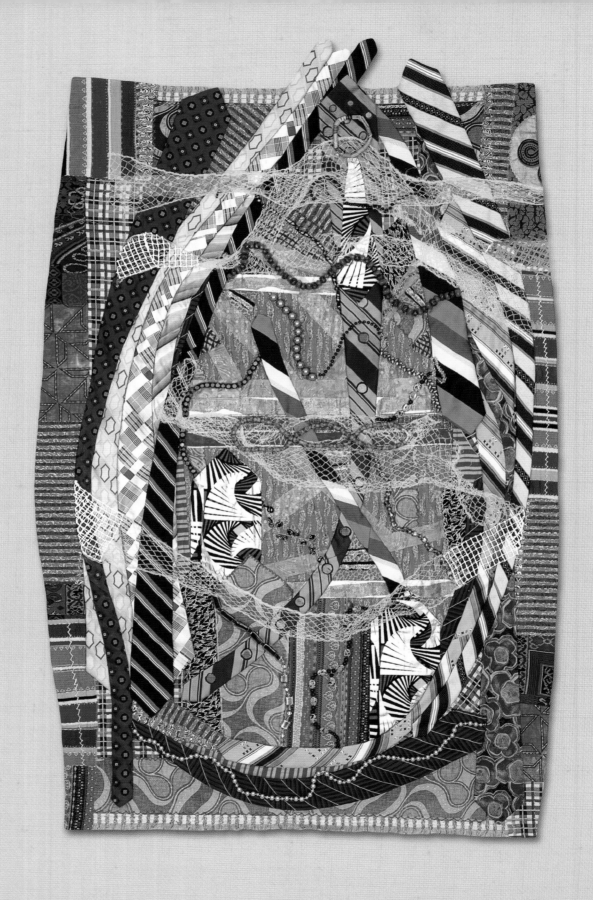

Universal Matrix:
The Binding Force That Unites Us

Universal Matrix:
The Binding Force That Unites Us

Mayota Hill I Pittsburgh, Pennsylvania I 2009 I
52 x 44 inches (132 x 112 cm) I Neckties, beads,
ribbon, embroidery thread, boning, grocery
produce netting I Improvised with glue and
nonspecific stitchery I *Photo by Chas. E. and
Mary B. Martin*

I asked myself: What most significant common factor do the people of this country and of the world have that might encourage them to consider themselves as parts of a whole coming together to exist as one powerful global unit? It came to me that Mother Earth is the holder of this commonality. She is the matrix in which all people of the universe are born and reside, and we as a people are siblings sharing this one and the same birth mother—Mother Earth. This work symbolizes Mother Earth as the common matrix for the birthplace of all humanity.

Ties outline the formation of the matrix and represent the male protective agent that safeguards her, her residing children, and ourselves. The bottom tie holds and shields the strand of pearls that denotes the foundation of the body of her mass. Her inner parts, composed of strands of beads, ribbons, and other connecting elements, represent the linking of her children. She forms a strong and bold structure of oneness within her space.

Janice E. Hobson
Starburst II

I was inspired to make *Starburst II* to celebrate the election of President Barrack Obama.

Every fifty years or so, in a galaxy about the size of the Milky Way, the universe experiences a rebirth known as a starburst or supernova, resulting in the formation of luminous young stars.

A new president represents a rebirth, an opportunity for a new beginning. The election victory of President Barrack Obama is America's opportunity for a fresh start, new ideas, change, and a rebirth.

Starburst II

Janice E. Hobson I Chicago, Illinois I 2009 I 54 x 39 inches (137 x 99 cm) I Commercial cotton, felt, polyester batting, variegated threads, beads, found objects, textile and acrylic paint, and wire I Appliquéd, embellished, embroidered, fused, and quilted I *Photo by Frederick O'Neal*

Lawana Holland-Moore
Wildest Dreams

"We're one and can work together. This is wonderful . . . isn't it beautiful?" My eighty-five-year-old grandmother's words could not ring more true in a time when so many need this bit of hope in their lives. My piece represents my ancestors—my maternal and paternal grandfathers and great-grandfathers, respectively—who had the hope to believe that something like this, so beyond their wildest dreams, could happen.

Wildest Dreams

Lawana Holland-Moore I Fairmont Heights, Maryland I 2008
I 26.5 x 23 inches (67 x 58 cm) I Commercial and hand-painted
cotton, bespoke tailoring wools, wax pastels I Hand painted,
fused appliqué I Hand and machine embroidered I
Photo by Chas. E. and Mary B. Martin

Through hard work and
sacrifice each of us can
pursue our individual
dreams

but still come
together as one
American family

to ensure that
the next
generation

can pursue
their dreams
as well

— B. Obama

The Path of Unyielding Hope

Sonji Hunt | Riverhills, Wisconsin | 2008 |
36 x 34 inches (91 x 86 cm) | Hand-dyed
cotton | Machine stitched | *Photo by
Chas. E. and Mary B. Martin*

Sonji Hunt

The Path of Unyielding Hope

For most of my adult life, people have said to me that my hopefulness is foolish or naive.

Barack Obama consistently speaks of "unyielding hope." Each day I say to myself, "I have hope." I feel it in my chest. Often, I need to say it throughout the day . . . "I have hope." Hope that the world will be a better place because of my deliberate, thoughtful daily actions toward others and my environment. Hope that others will do the same.

Hope travels an uncharted path and has many identities. It cannot stop itself from spreading or be something desperate or angry or greedy. It must be honest, adaptable, unfamiliar, and sometimes uneasy in order to be a change maker for us all on every level. The path of hope is unyielding. Hope is everything.

Charlotte Hunter
Gallery of Presidents

When the constitution was drafted, marriage between an African man and an American woman was outlawed. Our forefathers could not conceive that over 225 years later, an African American president would preside and reside at the big White House built by slaves.

During the sixties era, Americans, both ebony and ivory, fought bravely to obtain voting rights for African Americans. Could we imagine that merely fifty years later, President Barack Obama would join the Gallery of Presidents? "My country 'tis of thee, sweet land of liberty, of thee we can truly sing." A new generation of Americans can wave the Star-Spangled Banner high and say, "Yes We Can."

Gallery of Presidents

Charlotte Hunter I Cincinnati, Ohio I 2009 I 50 x 53 inches (127 x 135 cm) I Cotton, found objects I Machine pieced and quilted I *Photo by Chas. E. and Mary B. Martin*

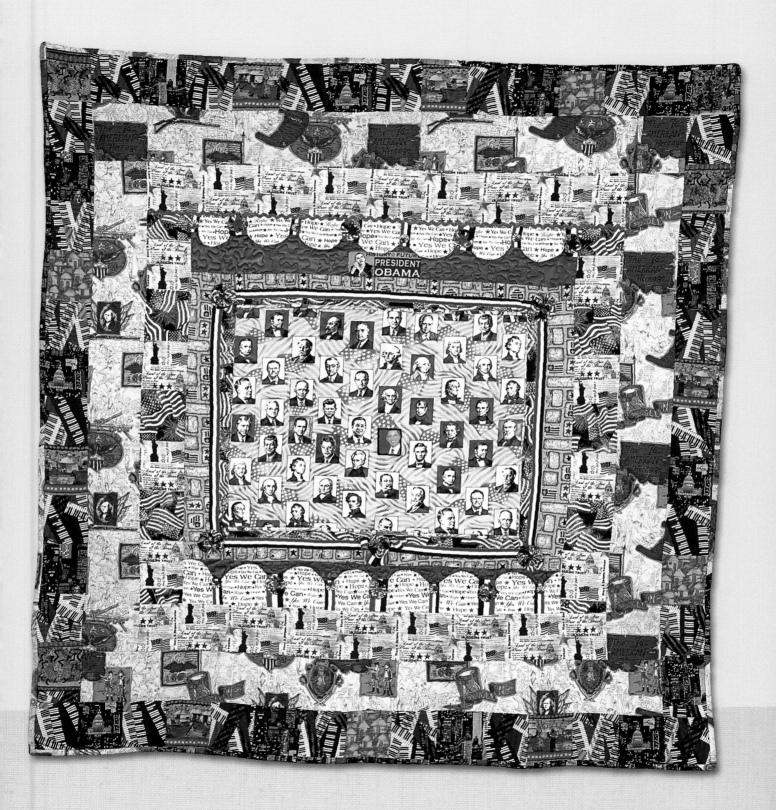

Lynette S. Jackson
The Obama Streak of Lightening

Traditional quilters have always used the craft to pay homage to monumental events. One need only read a list of quilt names to know this: *Tippecanoe and Tyler Too*, *Lincoln's Log Cabin* and *54-40 or Fight* are but a few traditional quilt names. I wanted to add a name to the list. *The Obama Streak of Lightening* combines a traditional patchwork Streak of Lightning with the appliquéd O symbol block. As Americans, we each bring our own "fabric" to the patchwork of America. Together we are as inextricably linked as the parts of a finished quilt; pieced together by country and quilted together by our shared experiences. Each of our cultures binds us together to create that "quilt" we call America.

My feelings about President Obama manifested themselves in *The Obama Streak of Lightening*. I used the traditional Streak of Lightning because the Obama presidency is as rare and substantial as a lightning strike. Indeed, it has been analogous to a lightning storm: powerful, breathtakingly full of energy, and . . . electric!

The Obama Streak of Lightening is what I created to juxtapose two things: the honor of being an American and the satisfaction of living through history.

The Obama Streak of Lightening

Lynette S. Jackson I Marietta, Georgia I 2009 I 78 x 78 inches (198 x 198 cm) I Cotton batiks, cotton batting I Hand pieced, appliquéd, and quilted I *Photo by Chas. E. and Mary B. Martin*

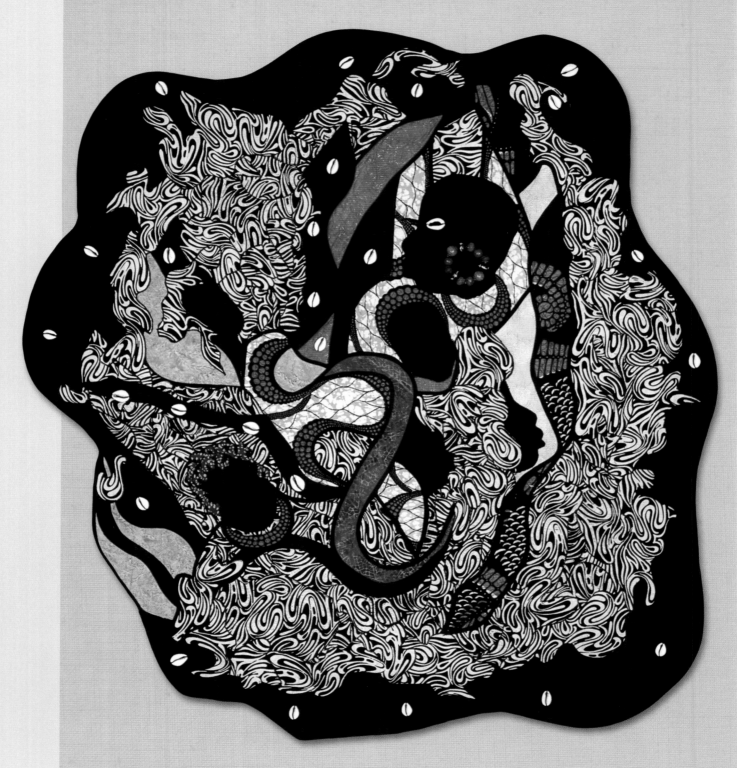

The Journey Forward

Marla Jackson I Lawrence, Kansas I 2009 I 43 x 35 inches (109 x 89 cm) I Cotton batiks, African cowrie shells, bias tape, wooden beads I Reverse machine appliquéd and machine quilted I *Photo courtesy of the artist*

Marla Jackson
The Journey Forward

"From the first moment a woman dared to speak that hope—dared to believe that the American Dream was meant for her too—ordinary women have taken on extraordinary odds to give their daughters the chance for something else; for a life more equal, more free, and filled with more opportunity than they ever had. In so many ways we have succeeded, but in so many areas we have much work left to do."

—Barack Obama, November 10, 2005

My abstract use of thematic imagery in the quilt *The Journey Forward* draws upon the use of fabric moving through the portraits of African American women. *The Journey Forward* reflects motion; the movement and the complex dynamics of women's lives. I wanted to create a visual image of the spectacular strength and bravery of women who are moving forward.

Whether it is the appreciation of beauty, evidence of excellence, steadfast hope, or the call of courage, the humanity of women is undeniable. In the midst of never-ending demands of society, family, or careers, women seek justice for themselves.

The Journey Forward is one that requires wisdom and temperance as we forgive past trespasses and welcome civil engagements. My quilt demonstrates that, amid the swirling motion of our active lives, individuality is recognized as unique portraits that emerge intelligently and with distinct vitality.

Joy-Lily
Help, Hope & Hallelujah!

I expected to get tired of election news stories long before November 2008, but I never did! I was fascinated to learn how caucuses work, to learn that Democratic and Republican delegates are allotted by different rules, and by the cliffhanging Democratic primary race. The impact of the Internet fundraising drive, the massive grassroots organization, long-distance cell-calling parties, competing polls, and the amazing surge of human energy that made Obama's campaign so successful kept me tethered to my radio all year. My quilt is inspired by the whole glorious, chaotic process. It is dedicated, with gratitude, to the many, hard-working volunteers of the Obama campaign.

As well as making art quilts, I create art cloth. I printed this uber-dot fabric years ago. I'd planned to cut it into squares and reassemble them as a simple grid quilt. One night in October, I got a visual image of random red stripes slashing those squares. Visions from my muse are rare, so I immediately started slicing the fabric to add those stripes. Blue and yellow stripes followed. Gradually, this quilt became a graphic metaphor for the election: the blocks of dots became party HQs; the stripes crisscrossing the quilt spoke to me of volunteers communicating and traveling across the United States; the yellow dots might be those pesky undecided voters; the upswing in the big red swish was the Sarah Palin effect. The whole work represents the overlaid, seemingly scattered, yet highly purposeful energy of the presidential campaign. I especially wanted to evoke the holding-your-breath hope of those last few days before the election, overlaid with the heart-opening joy of celebration, shared by so many of us as Mr. Obama made his acceptance speech.

Help, Hope & Hallelujah!

Joy-Lily I San Francisco, California I 2008 I 40 x 50 inches (102 x 127 cm) I Cottons I Hand screened by artist, machine pieced and appliquéd I *Photo by Chas. E. and Mary B. Martin*

Niambi Kee
O Is for Obama

This piece was done in 2007 during the campaign.

Its purpose is to illustrate Obama's boundless energy, exuberance, and complexity!

O Is for Obama

Niambi Kee I Hayward, California I 2007 I 39 x 38 inches (99 x 97 cm) I
Cotton and rayon thread I Pieced and appliquéd I *Collection of William
A. Savage* I *Photo by Chas. E. and Mary B. Martin*

Peg Keeney
We the People: Together We Can

I live in Harbor Springs, Michigan, which is located on the shore of Lake Michigan in the northwestern part of the Lower Peninsula. As an art quilter, I am inspired by my surroundings and the events that touch my life. I tend to work intuitively, building each piece like a collage, using the basic elements of a quilt. My canvasses combine hand-dyed, commercial, stamped, and painted fabrics; digitally altered photographs; and a variety of embellishments to achieve my vision.

I began working full-time as an artist in 2001. I have been a juror and curator. I am a professional member and board member of Studio Art Quilt Associates and serve as chair of its Exhibition Committee. The process of the 2008 presidential campaigns and subsequent historic election of Barack Obama excited me as has no other election in recent history. His calm, inspiring words and promises have brought hope to millions of Americans. My quilt celebrates the idea that we, as Americans, can put aside our partisan differences and work together. Yes, we can, with determination, work together to create a world that will be a better place for our children and grandchildren.

On the quilt are lines from Obama's speeches:

At this defining moment change has come to America.

This is our moment, to promote peace, restore prosperity, and reclaim the American dream.

Let us summon a new spirit of patriotism, service, and responsibility.

We resolve to work together . . . our union can be perfected.

We the People

Peg Keeney I Harbor Springs, Michigan I 2009 I 36 x 36 inches (91 x 91 cm) I
Cotton, photo transfer I Appliquéd and machine quilted I *Photo by Chas. E. and Mary B. Martin.*

The Journey Ends

Gloria Kellon I Shaker Heights, Ohio I 2008 I 69 x 47.5 inches (175 x 121 cm) I Cotton photo transfer, rayon thread I Fused appliquéd, thread painted, machine embroidered, and quilted I *Photo by Chas. E. and Mary B. Martin*

Gloria Kellon
The Journey Ends

Those who sought freedom and those who helped freedom seekers knew the Underground Railroad as a means to an end. The end being freedom— a chance to live a life guided by their own choices.

Louis Stokes' efforts to pass the National UGRR Network to Freedom Amendments Act of 2007 demanded that I stitch this quilt to honor all those involved in Civil War history. Unfortunately, it seems that, even in modern times, safe houses and conductors are needed for opportunities and justice.

The Journey Ends parallels two journeys: Obama's election trail to the office of the president, a goal some said never would be achieved, and the UGRR as a vehicle for change. Obama's triumph in the election mirrored those slaves who followed the North Star seeking freedom and who finally achieved their freedom in Canada. Perhaps with this election, all citizens will become first-class citizens and know the meaning of liberty and justice for all.

Without plan or reason, I stitched the binding of this quilt while watching the election returns. When it was announced that Obama had won, I looked down at the quilt and thought of all those who had traveled the UGRR. I thought of the millions who had died and the lesser number who had made it to freedom. The impact of what had just happened was powerful. The freedom seekers' journey had ended. They could rise up and take their places because the journey had come to an end, but with a new beginning. Let us pray that our future will continue to grow in a positive path. Obama is the change factor.

The Jacob's Ladder patchwork background was chosen because this pattern, it is said, was used as a safety signal for slaves. Fabric photo prints, African and batik fabrics, fused appliqué, machine embroidery, and thread painting were combined to honor the UGRR sites of northeastern Ohio.

Sharon Kerry-Harlan
DIS

The title refers to the cultural understanding of the popular verb *dis*, meaning to disrespect. Hundreds of other "dis" possibilities exist: disavowed, disempowered, disenfranchised, disgraced, dishonored, dismissed, disowned, etc. Such an overarching meaning for *dis* defines the sacrificial lives of African American men; from auction block to cellblock to shot block, these men have earned respect that they never received. Barack Obama's historic selection as the first African American president has raised the expectations of Americans—ushering in global changes that bring hope for a new age. Not surprisingly, today, because of Barack Obama's election as the forty-fourth U.S. president, black men can feel themselves redeemed!

DIS

Sharon Kerry-Harlan I Wauwatosa, Wisconsin I 2009 I 40 x 30.5 inches (102 x 77 cm) I Discharge dyed, reverse appliquéd, and free-motion quilted I *Photo by Chas. E. and Mary B. Martin*

Beverly Huggins Kirk
Transcendence

A clash of colors . . . bright and flowing shapes . . . slanted, curved, and moving up, down, and across. Lifted heads, giving hands, smiling faces, global women at work and play, gleaming eyes filled with hope. My quilt gives expression to my search for transcendence.

The Pledge of Allegiance and words of liberty speak from the blue fabric. I dared to believe "and justice for all." Why was there a Trail of Tears or Holocaust or 1876 Dred Scott decision? Was there "equal justice under the law" when Ada Sipuel Fisher sought admission the University of Oklahoma in 1946? Was transcendence achieved in the 1958 sit-ins by Clara Luper and Nancy Davis?

I have memories of Olympians' black fists raised in protest, of titles being stripped from Ali and Hurricane Carter. A slow, deliberate march as we woefully sang "We Shall Overcome." Assassinations attempted and assassinations carried out. The Tulsa Riot, the Oklahoma City bombing, the attacks of September 11. Wars and rumors of wars . . . my brothers served in the Viet Nam era; in 2002 I stood and did not cry as my only son, nineteen years of age, stepped onto a Fort Sill bus bound for Iraq. Repeated pain has been inflicted by drive-by shootings, domestic violence, and drug abuse. I've been sometimes doubtful, but always hoping for a vehicle of mercy and justice that would offer transcendence above such things in the United States and abroad.

America now has a human representative, a commander-in-chief in DC who is uniquely gifted and qualified to exhibit an aura of transcendence as he serves from January 2009 to December 2012. His journey is our journey. While Malcolm X exhorted "by any means possible" and Martin called us to nonviolent protest, President Obama is the blending and balance our world needs! May he and his family live long and live well. I believe his mother-in-law is a jewel in hiding—a woman experienced in transcending.

Transcendence

Beverly Huggins Kirk | Oklahoma City, Oklahoma | 2009 | 80 x 70 inches (203 x 178 cm) | African cotton, commercial cotton | Patchwork, machine appliquéd and quilted | *Photo courtesy of the artist*

Anita Knox
The Guardians

The Guardians is a continuation of my Vessel series, which is nearing completion. It is an appropriate quilt for the tribute to and celebration of our first African American president of the United States of America. The vessels on the quilt hold African proverbs (in recognition of our African roots) and two quotes by Franklin D. Roosevelt (whom I read President Obama admires). The vessel is important to all world cultures. Its purpose, while utilitarian in design and function, is also a significant record of the traditions, iconography, and spirit of a culture. This quilt is inspired and designed as a symbol of that idea.

The Guardians

Anita Holman Knox I Fort Worth, Texas I 2008 I
36 x 34 inches I Hand-dyed cotton, beads, and
paper I Pieced, appliquéd, and hand and machine
quilted I *Photo by Chas. E. and Mary B. Martin*

That won.
'08

That Won

Carol Krueger I Louisville, Colorado I 2008 I 12.5 x 15.5 inches (32 x 39 cm) I Glass seed beads, cotton background, imported cottons from India and Guatemala, cotton welt I Hand beaded, digitized computer monogramming, and machine welt I *Collection of Joyce Jewell and Wilfred Brunner* I *Photo by artist*

Carol Krueger

That Won

The 2008 presidential election meant high visibility for my home state of Colorado. The fact that Colorado was considered an important swing state brought excitement and a deep feeling of angst to the Mile-High City. Colorado had traditionally been a red state; it would take some effort to turn it around. As the battle between McCain and Obama raged, Coloradans were inundated with visits from both parties and a barrage of ads from both campaigns. Special-interest groups created their own bizarre negative commercials, which only fueled the public's hostility. I witnessed a near fistfight in the parking lot of my local Costco. Enough was enough. I needed a creative project.

In order to quell my anxiety, I decided to create a beaded image of Barack Obama. This portrait contains around fourteen-thousand glass seed beads that were hand sewn onto a lightweight canvas base. Approximately one hundred hours of beading went into the project. Much of the sewing was accomplished while listening to my primary sources of news, *The Daily Show with Jon Stewart* and *The Colbert Report*.

Of course, I also tuned into the presidential debates. This is where I got the idea for the title of my piece. The title was graciously provided by Senator McCain as he condescendingly referred to Senator Obama as "that one." I immediately saw the term *that won* in my mind's eye, and I knew instinctively that McCain would regret the day he used those careless words. I devised a sort of monogrammed campaign button to embellish my finished portrait.

On October 26, 2008, my husband and I brought our two children to see Barack Obama speak in Denver. As I looked out onto the sea of the one hundred thousand or so devoted individuals who had poured through the streets and lined the steps to the state capitol on that glorious autumn day, I felt that a change truly was in the air.

Hope Rising

Deborah Lacativa I Lawrenceville, Georgia I 2008 I 18 x 44 inches (46 x 112 cm) I Commercial and hand-dyed cottons, silk, flannel, beads I
Machine pieced and quilted I *Photo by Chas. E. and Mary B. Martin*

Deborah Lacativa
Hope Rising

The seed for my quilt reaches back to July 2004. I was visiting my parents in New York. My Dad is a World War II veteran, and his worldview and politics have been at odds with my own since the late sixties. As was our habit, I stayed up late to keep him company while he watched television. It was getting late when he stopped channel surfing to watch the Democratic National Convention "and see what them damned Democrats were up to now," as if he were a spy in an enemy camp.

I was on the couch with my arm thrown over my eyes, when the keynote speaker was introduced. The crowd went crazy, as if Elvis were swinging in from the rafters, and Barack Obama began to speak. My dad stopped muttering epithets under his breath, I sat up, and we both leaned into the broadcast, listening intently.

I was stunned and amazed by Obama's forthrightness, sincerity, and eloquence, but it was the message he brought that rang in the air like a bell. When Mr. Obama finished speaking, I turned to my dad. Struggling to contain the emotion I felt, I simply said, "He is going to be the next president of the United States." He knew I expected him to make a racial comment, but my father could only reply disdainfully, "He's too young." He understood the truth in that moment as well as I did.

I started this piece on my birthday in October of 2008 as a personal statement of the quiet and fearful hope I had for our country and Barack Obama. When making it, I felt the need to protect my hopefulness like a candle in the wind. My artistic effort was small and dark, the spotlight of the moon a focus on which to hang that hope.

I am deeply grateful to the American voting public, which set aside fear and elected a leader with a different perspective on the challenges this county faces. Now, as a people, the hope is that we can put away childish things—the endless gluttony of self-concern and self-indulgence that has falsely driven our culture and economy—and work together to restore our country's self-respect.

Viola Burley Leak

Celebrating Barack Obama: America's First Afro-American President

America's First Afro-American President

The left side of this quilt is predominately black and white. It is the side of crisis. It represents financial decline, war, and black-and-white racial issues, along with slavery. The top left of the quilt represents Obama breaking part of the chains of racism. The black-and-white figure represents a biracial Obama holding the world, and hope is symbolized by the rising phoenix. At the top center of the quilt, Obama has ascended to the White House with the largest star of the forty-four resting above. The open hands at the bottom right are releasing all forty-four of the presidential stars.

Martin Luther King Jr. and the American flag rest at the lower portion of the quilt, recalling the promise that we shall overcome adversity. Written with matching color thread are words from Maya Angelou's poem "Still I Rise."

Celebrating Barack Obama: America's First Afro-American President

Viola Burley Leak I Washington, DC I 2008 I 36 x 36 inches (91 x 91 cm) I Cotton, velvet I Raw-edge hand appliquéd, collaged, machine quilted I *Photo by Chas. E. and Mary B. Martin*

Change, Exchange and Vision

***Change, Exchange and Vision* is a visual discussion of Obama's rise to the presidency** and the transferring of Republican-made burdens to the Democratic Party. Some of Obama's visions are presented in the portrait area of the piece. How he directs his visions will be revealed in time. My quilt depicts a black-and-white figure of Obama as a biracial president, using black, white, and gray to punctuate the idea of the president's mixed-race ancestry.

The three raised hands are symbolic of taking the oath of office. An abstract window shape next to the portrait of Lincoln represents Obama's openness to change. The changing shape of the dollar falls from the area of vision and directs the eye to three Republican elephants, which carry a house too close to the flames, thus foreclosure; money that is burning and being consumed; and a war tank with planes and destruction from above. All the burdens of the elephants are being transferred through the fire to the Democratic donkey. The intermittent red arrows show issues moving in different directions.

Change, Exchange and Vision

Viola Burley Leak I Washington, DC I 2009 I 54 x 45 inches (137 x 114 cm) I Cotton, lamé I Machine quilted I *Photo courtesy of the artist*

Cynthia Lockhart
Mr. President

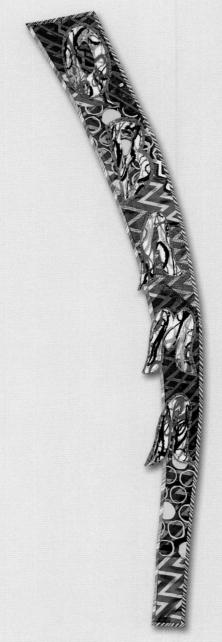

I truly believe that we as a people witnessed the awesome power of God in motion, and that God orchestrated the Obama journey to the White House. God weaved a perfect pattern. He put together people of different ethnic backgrounds, created opportunities that developed over a span of a lifetime. God sent the Holy Spirit to dance, whisper, shout, cry, and articulate the coming of this event. I was one of the persons who heard the whisper from the Holy Spirit: "He is the one." Oh no, the making of the Obama presidency was not an overnight phenomenon but the result of strategic planning from the Master.

As I look back over the journey of my life and the path toward becoming who I am, it has been an evolution of change. I now see that America has also progressed. Through a new voice, we can sing a new song about the audacity of hope in America. I am so awestruck and grateful that I had the great fortune to participate in and witness this transformation. There are important dates in my life that are precious, such as births, deaths, graduations, and now specifically November 4, 2008. I, along with my family and billions of others, will always remember that date in November of 2008 when we stood in unity. I will have that memory always of how we celebrated the paradigm shift in America and in the world as a result of the election of Barack Obama as the forty-fourth president of the United States of America.

Mr. President

Cynthia Lockhart I Cincinnati, Ohio I 2009 I 65 x 48 inches (165 x 122 cm) I Upholstery, boiled wool, snakeskin, cotton, linen, batiks, netting, lace, mesh, and metallic trims I Appliquéd, pieced, bias quilted, 3-D sculpted, and draped I *Photo by Jay Yocis*

133

Cynthia Lockhart
Spirit of Victory

Symbols represented in this quilt are abstractions of being moved by the spirit of the Lord. This was God's plan; miracles still take place; all the signs and wonders were aligned. The Obama movement swept the world and held us mesmerized. The images in the quilt glimmer, fly, and spin, depicting the emotion intended for such a time as this. People who got caught up in the experience know what I speak of. Multitudes of people stood peacefully for hours waiting and wanting. Majorities of people were on one accord. They answered a call to hope for a change and to believe that it was possible for a nation to transform by way of a vote. The veil had been lifted and the achievement passed on to an upbeat, intelligent, confident man of excellence.

The victory was so powerful. Some people stared in amazement; others, like Jesse Jackson, could not hold back tears of joy. In addition, many danced, shouted, and prayed. I believe the presidential victory of 2008 was celebrated beyond the earth's atmosphere and into the heavens. For me, President Obama is representative of a brilliant light, a beacon of hope, and the ever presence of inspiration. He is an exceptional role model as a leader and a family man. The victory is just the beginning. Continue to pray for love, unity, and prosperity for his presidency and our nation.

Spirit of Victory

Cynthia Lockhart I Cincinnati, Ohio I 2009 I 49 x 46 inches (124 x 117 cm) I Batik fabric, hand-dyed upholstery, cotton, lace, organza, mesh, Angelina fibers, braids, beads, buttons, beading, stones, straw tubing, brass ornaments, CDs, leather, and feathers I Appliquéd, hand and machine stitched, bias quilted, hand stamped, and hand painted I *Photo by Jay Yocis*

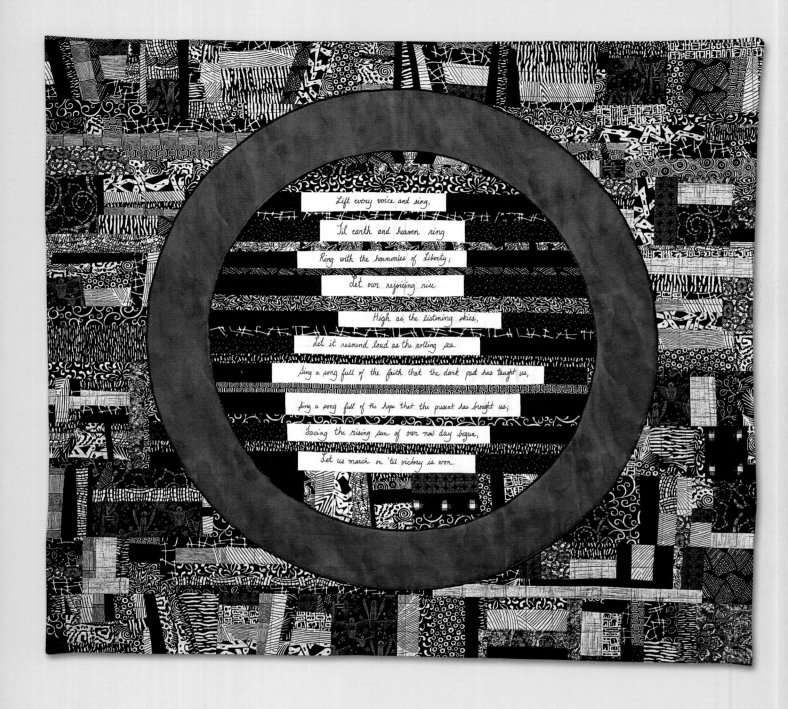

The quilt text reads:

Lift every voice and sing,

'Til earth and heaven ring

Ring with the harmonies of Liberty;

Let our rejoicing rise

High as the listening skies,

Let it resound loud as the rolling sea.

Sing a song full of the faith that the dark past has taught us,

Sing a song full of the hope that the present has brought us;

Facing the rising sun of our new day begun,

Let us march on 'til victory is won.

Lift Every Voice and Sing for Obama

Jeanne Marklin | Williamstown, Massachusetts | 2009 | 50 x 54 inches (127 x 137 cm) | Cotton fabrics, chenille yarn, cotton threads, fabric pen | Appliquéd and machine quilted | *Photo courtesy of the artist*

Jeanne Marklin

Lift Every Voice and Sing for Obama

Sing a song full of the faith that the dark past has taught us,

The years leading up to the election of President Barack Obama were filled with fear for the loss of civil liberties, our international reputation, and the safety of my son—a soldier who served in Iraq—and others who served in a war that never should have happened.

The Obama campaign was a positive and empowering campaign, and working at the polls in New Hampshire on Election Day was a moving experience. Watching people come in on crutches, in wheelchairs, and with oxygen tanks made me proud of our electoral process. The first-time voters were so excited to be counted as full-fledged Americans.

So many fears were overcome that day. A weight was lifted from my, and our nation's, shoulders.

When thinking about how to express these feelings in one quilt, my consciousness was flooded with thoughts of the sacrifices of those who had died due to slavery, lynchings, activism, and service to our country. In reviewing a book on African American history, I came across the hymn "Lift Every Voice and Sing" and felt chills at how well it expressed the moment. It became the centerpiece of the artwork.

The black and white fabrics were sewn and cut into varying shapes to represent the tumultuous history that led to the election of a great African American. The red "O" is for Obama, and also to represent the circle of support that was there for those who believed in equality and fought for it. The hymn was one of the many songs that were a source of strength on the long road, and it still represents the hope that President Obama has brought to American citizens.

Gwen Maxwell-Williams

Obama— The Promise

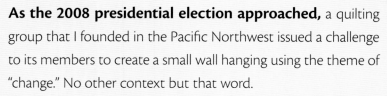

As the 2008 presidential election approached, a quilting group that I founded in the Pacific Northwest issued a challenge to its members to create a small wall hanging using the theme of "change." No other context but that word.

As I pondered what to do, the greatest impact I saw for the United States and the world was the image of a black man who influenced people from all walks of life, religious persuasions, varying economic levels, and rural and urban environments. They saw his vision for change and hope and adopted it as their mantra too. He inspired in all of us the belief that through unity and hope for the future, we could and would make things happen and create a better, more sustainable world for all of us.

The colors chosen for this piece represent a bright future for our country. The open format represents the transparency, openness, and promise that we all anticipate as a new era begins for American citizens and the world.

Obama—The Promise

Gwen Maxwell-Williams I Redmond, Washington I 2009 I 25 x 25 inches (64 x 64 cm) I Cottons and raw-edge appliqué I *Photo by Mark Fry*

Barbara Ann McCraw

Growing a New America

As I sat in my studio, my granddaughter Maddie playing close by, I began to make sketches for this quilt. Many times before, I had sat down to make drawings but rejected each one in turn. Nothing seemed to be right enough to express my feelings about our new president. I could only think about his two little girls, and my past.

As a little girl, I lived in a Chicago tenement with my large family. My little sister and I were the youngest. We overheard the whispers about racism, but Lessie and I didn't know anything about that. We laughed and played and were so very happy. Lessie died when she was nineteen.

As I watched the election on television, the strongest memory was of my mother. She was seventy-seven years old and had broken her leg. We didn't have a car, but she insisted on getting to the polling place anyway. As I walked close beside her, I fussed about how stubborn she was. That's when she recounted old stories about how difficult it had been for blacks to vote, about how many had lost their lives for the privilege. She fussed right back at me, saying, "Don't you ever forget what it means for us to have a voice in this country."

As I looked up at Maddie, a vision for my quilt began to form. It was a childlike, joyous vision of two sisters laughing and playing. However, this time it was Sasha and Malia. I even allowed Maddie to help me draw it.

That I have the privilege of living in this country at this time is indeed a joy. At the moment Barack Obama was elected president, I'm sure Mommy was somewhere shouting, "Hallelujah, our day has come."

Growing a New America

Barbara Ann McCraw I Denton, Texas I 2009 I 38 x 42 inches (97 x 107 cm) I Cotton fabrics, cotton and metallic threads, crystals, fabric inks I Machine appliquéd and quilted I *Photo by Ernest McCraw*

In My Lifetime . . . A Path of Injustice, Accomplishments, and a Victory Declared

Harriette A. Meriwether I Pittsburgh, Pennsylvania I 2009 I 77 x 80 inches (196 x 203 cm) I Cotton, monofil thread I
Appliquéd, pieced, machine quilted by Sandra German I *Photo by Chas. E. and Mary B. Martin*

Harriette A. Meriwether

In My Lifetime . . .
A Path of Injustice, Accomplishments, and a Victory Declared

Growing up in the South, I was aware of my kinship to Africa and the forced migration of Africans to the United States, and I was aware of slavery, lynching, segregation, and the emptiness in the eyes of my grandparents. This work of art documents some of the emotions, events, and experiences that have impacted my life and brought me to one of the proudest moments yet: the election of Barack Obama, an African American, as forty-fourth president of the United States of America.

The colors and design chosen for my quilt have significance. Red conveys intensity, depth, torture, shame, adversity, and brokenness. The black and white circles refer to the imposed punishment and pain directed at blacks by white America. The circles denote the extent and duration of the suffering. The text declares and confirms that blacks have always been a giving and capable people. The hands reach out in distress, and in celebration of all we have encountered. This quilt also highlights some of the contributions and accomplishments of African Americans. Each block of the inner border is done in a liberated Log Cabin pattern, representing the simple dwellings most African Americans called home. President Barack Obama's image at the top of the inner border gives me hope that real change has begun.

This quilt is intended to tell a story; celebrate the lives and history of African Americans; salute the many martyrs, both men and women, who stood for justice; and honor President Barack Obama. This quilt is dedicated to three women whose spirit lifted and inspired me: Harriet Tubman, Rosa Parks, and Rosette B. Alford (my mother).

Ed Johnetta Miller

And I Embrace All Cultures

My improvisational quilt is composed of fabrics from Africa, Asia, Europe, and the Americas. The pieces come together in unity and harmony to create a whole. At this historic period in our nation's history, it is my hope that the election of America's first African American president brings unity to the people of the United States.

And I Embrace All Cultures

Ed Johnetta Miller I Hartford, Connecticut I 2008 I 33 x 35 inches (84 x 89 cm) I Silk and rayon fabric from Africa, Japan, France, and the United States I Machine pieced and quilted I *Photo by Chas. E. and Mary B. Martin*

Helen Murrell
At This Moment

I love using symbols in my quilts. I find a peaceful presence with the past, knowing that generations have used the symbols as a means of expression in their art and daily lives. This is a quilt with many symbols. The central theme is *sankofa*, an *adinkra* symbol, which is portrayed as a bird moving forward while looking backward. It teaches us that we should learn from the past so that we can move forward. President Obama has the intelligence and talent to take what lessons the past has shown us to understand the present and to prepare for a promising future.

The rectangular sets of dots are forty-four in number to commemorate the forty-fourth president. The side panel on the right has the word *hope* repeated to represent the hope that we all feel, now that we have elected this president. The three triangles symbolize important women in the life of the president—his grandmother, mother, and wife—all having strong influences on his life. All three have given him strength and a strong sense of nurturing, which are important qualities in a great leader. It is my belief that President Barack Obama will acknowledge the past and cultivate a better future.

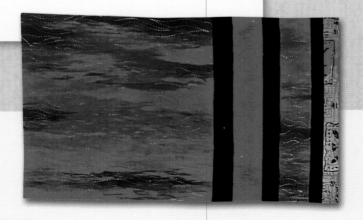

At This Moment

Helen Murrell I Cleveland Heights, Ohio I 2009 I 49 x 40 inches (124 x 102 cm) I Cotton fabrics, cotton batting I Discharge dyed, screen printed, pieced, and free-motion quilted I *Photo by Chas. E. and Mary B. Martin*

Helen Murrell
Free Flowing

Like an abstract painting, which when viewed from any direction presents itself as a masterpiece of complex patterns yet is seemingly simple and flowing with ease, I wanted this quilt to reflect the personality and character of President Obama. His calmness under crisis is symbolized by the quiet, rhythmic waves of quilting. The texture of this cloth reminds me of his multifaceted character, logical thinking, and ability to control with calmness and yet with strength. I used rhythmic stitches; the dyes flow with strong color to echo his intelligence, the way he analyzes situations, and his high energy. This quilt is an expression of President Barack Obama's strengths: dynamism, empathy, and resourcefulness.

I am very proud that we have an African American president, but it is with greater pride that I rejoice that we have elected a president with grand credentials.

Free Flowing

Helen Murrell I Cleveland Heights, Ohio I 2009 I 25 x 40 inches (64 x 102 cm) I Hand-dyed African fabrics, cotton fabric dyed by artist, cotton batting, polyester thread I Curved pieced and free-motion quilted I *Photo by Chas. E. and Mary B. Martin*

Sandra Noble

Obama Lights the World with Hope

During the last administration, the world viewed the United States as a distrustful, overbearing bully. Some high-ranking U.S. officials perpetuated hate, divisiveness, and fear within and outside of the borders of our country. Darkness and disillusionment seemed to surround the United States and the world. Many powerful world officials and countries once viewed the United States as a leader and demonstrator of right and goodness.

I had serious concerns for our future, the disregard for human conditions, the war mongering, the racism, and our country being sold out from under us for the sake of the almighty dollar. Barack Obama, a man of intelligence, compassion, and respect for all, elected as the president of the United States, gave hope to the world and to me.

Obama brings us a sense of light and spirit, a sense that we can live in this world to-gether in peace with mutual respect; together we can ensure the future of this world. I created my quilt to represent the spirit of hope radiated by Obama for all the people of the world, not just those in the United States. I made the countries with a bright yellow fabric to show the light brought about by hope and because I think of the color as up-lifting and forward moving. Obama not only affected countries but also individuals, so I used gold lines and strips to spread the light across the different-colored faces that depict the various people of the world.

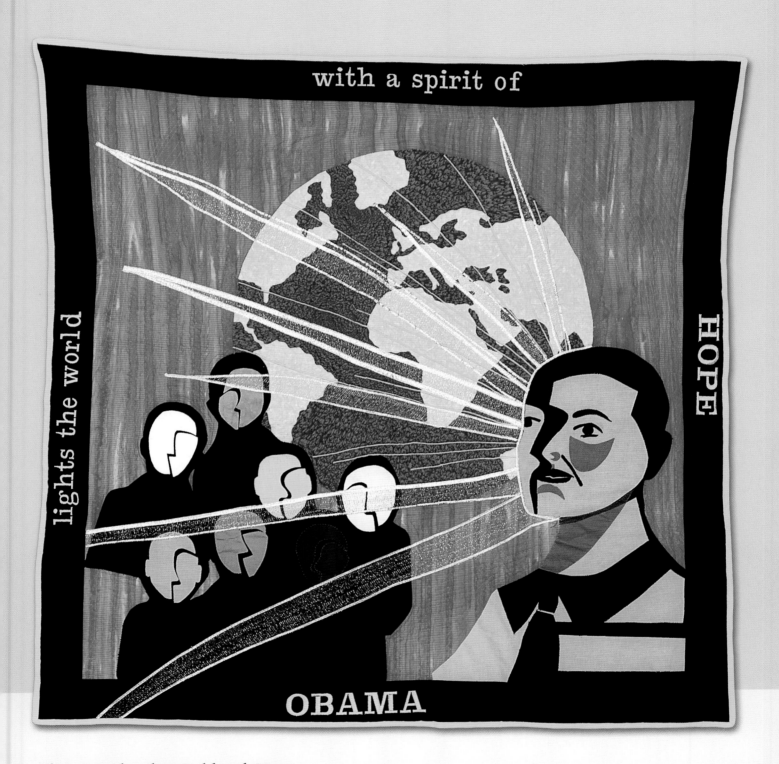

Obama Lights the World with Hope

Sandra Noble I Warrensville Heights, Ohio I 2009 I 44 x 44 inches (112 x 112 cm) I Cotton, gold netting, gold ribbon, organza I Machine appliquéd, fused, and embroidered I *Photo by Chas. E. and Mary B. Martin*

In the Shadow of Our Freedom

Charlotte O'Neal I Arusha, Tanzania I 2009 I 29 x 40 inches (74 x 102 cm) I Cotton, vinyl, velvet, cowrie shells, beads, found objects I Machine appliquéd and quilted I *Photo by Chas. E. and Mary B. Martin*

Charlotte O'Neal

In the Shadow of Our Freedom

Just as the historic election of President Barack Obama inspired great hope and pride and joy in the hearts of people around the world, we can have no doubt that the innumerable contributions and positive, powerful examples of African American women throughout communities in the United States must have provided thoughtful inspiration for President Obama as well. Women have always been in the forefront of our historical struggle for freedom and empowerment: from the women who claimed their freedom, breaking their chains of slavery to reclaim and build their lives; to the women who first had the opportunities for formal learning in historically black institutions in America; to the powerfully expressive and respected blues singers of the thirties and forties who boldly sang about lynchings and the oppression of poor people of color; to the women of the civil rights and Black Power movements of the sixties and seventies; to the African women in America who are in the forefront of the green movement of this millennium.

That boomerang of inspiration keeps rebounding, and we still dare to struggle and we STILL win—all in the shadow and blessings of our ancestors, where it all began!

Pixeladies (Deb Cashatt and Kris Sazaki)

The Picture Is Only Half the Story

We have been friends for thirty years, and we had never talked so much about an upcoming election as we did this past year. We were so fed up with the war in Iraq, with the chipping away of our civil rights, with an administration that didn't seem to care about America, much less the world. From the moment Barack Obama announced his candidacy, we sensed that maybe this time we might be witnessing something special. Obama is, we've noted with great relief, a thoughtful person who actually listens to people. And while it may now be a cliché to say it, just uttering the words "President Obama" gives us hope. How remarkable a reaction on Election Night, when we gathered with friends and neighbors. We all hugged and said to one another, "Yes, the world *will* be a better place."

Making a quilt in his honor, in America's honor, for taking this bold step forward, was a logical step for us. We knew, too, how we wanted to execute the project (quilting aside—we always jostle over that). We cut words and phrases out of magazines and newspapers and then glued them onto paper into the shape we wanted. Afterward, we scanned the resulting image into the computer, made color corrections, and printed it out onto one piece of cotton fabric. We thought this technique was apt for this particular quilt because so many Americans have been projecting their hopes and dreams onto Obama. We also knew we needed to read his words as well. The text to the left of Obama's head is taken from his speech on race, "A More Perfect Union," delivered on March 18, 2008, in Philadelphia, Pennsylvania. May we all work to form that more perfect union.

The Picture Is Only Half the Story

Pixeladies (Deb Cashatt and Kris Sazaki) | Cameron Park, California |
2009 | 41 x 28 inches (104 x 71 cm) | Custom-printed cotton, perle
cotton | Newspaper and magazine collage digitally printed on cotton
| *Photo by Chas. E. and Mary B. Martin*

Jacob's Ladder: The Opening of the Heart of America

Theresa D. Polley-Shellcroft I Victorville, California I 2008 I 25 x 30 inches (64 x 76 cm) I Cotton, tulle, glass beads, shells, brass bells, pewter charms I Pieced, appliquéd, and hand and machine quilted I *Photo by Chas. E. and Mary B. Martin*

Theresa D. Polley-Shellcroft

Jacob's Ladder:
The Opening of the Heart of America

I am a storyteller at heart. I choose to spin my yarns through fiber and the visual arts. I grew up in the fifties, living through the periods of Jim Crow, discrimination, and legal segregation, when the lynching of African American men was an ordinary occurrence.

The night of my high school baccalaureate, I elected to walk on a picket line to integrate a restaurant in my hometown. I continued to participate in the civil rights movement through my college years. It was beyond my imagination to think that we could have a president who is of African American descent. This is the first time in my life that I have felt a deep connection to this country, accepted as a full citizen, although my roots go back for over nine generations and beyond, as my heritage is African, Cherokee, and Dutch.

This quilt reflects my meditation upon the significance of Barack Obama's road to the presidency. When thinking about the meaning of this historic event, the words to the Negro spiritual "We are Climbing Jacob's Ladder" continually came to heart. The overall composition is made up of eight individual quilted sections hand stitched together. In vignettes—put together in the manner of Kente cloth, strip by strip, section by section—I have tried to capture the many layers of meaning in Obama's rise, which ultimately is the rise of all regardless of ethnic, religious, or racial background. *Jacob's Ladder* is the road to glory! The subject matter includes the symbolism from Jacob's dream (Genesis 28) and the song "We Are Climbing Jacob's Ladder."

Images of the Statue of Liberty, the U.S. Capitol, and the Lincoln Memorial represent the earthly institutions through which we realize the higher spiritual realm of freedoms for all. Obama inspires and represents this new spiritual direction for the world.

Tears for Water

Keisha Roberts I San Francisco, California I 2009 I 36 x 30 inches (91 x 76 cm) I Silk, cotton, decorative threads
I Machine stitched I *Photo courtesy of the artist*

Keisha Roberts

Tears for Water

For many, President Obama's "Yes We Can" campaign slogan became a mantra whose repetition reminded us that we, as Americans, can come together, reconcile our differences and disagreements, and trade tears shed during a turbulent past for soothing waters of a more hopeful present. Intentional variations in thread tension create small stitches of red—symbolic of our nation's experience of racial tension and strife—on the quilt surface, which represents loss and healing at this historical moment. The quilt interior contains Buddhist mantras for peace, healing, and compassion.

Sheryl Schleicher

Black & White in a Red State

This quilt was made as a gift for our Obama field organizer, David Glasgow. David left his job in Washington, DC, and joined the campaign in Missouri during the spring of 2008. During our first phone call, as he was recruiting volunteers, we asked how things were going. He said, "The first steps are the hardest." Hence the ladder on the quilt.

I tried to convey other memories of the 2008 campaign through traditional quilting elements: the Flying Geese block as coming together through David's hard work and Missouri's political shift to the left. The right was simple and traditional. The gold-splattered fabric is a reminder of the Obama billboard in Camden County that was vandalized with paint.

The "Obanda" came from my son Christopher. Barack Obama inspired both my sons to become politically active for the first time, and I am very proud of their efforts. If you look closely, you will see the words *Hope*, *Peace*, and *Dream* in the fabric. Those words weren't just "talking points." They had real meaning for those of us in the field, knocking on one million doors nationwide.

The goal for Camden County was to get 28 percent of the vote. Obama got 35 percent.

As Barack Obama said, "Change will not come if we wait for some other person or some other time. We are the ones we have been waiting for. We are the change that we seek."

Thank you, David, for making change happen!

Black & White in a Red State

Sheryl Schleicher I Lenexa, Kansas I 2008 I 42 x 48 inches (107 x 122 cm) I "Obanda" from Obama rally in Springfield, Missouri; commercial cottons I Machine pieced and quilted I *Collection of David Glasgow* I *Photo by Captured Moments*

They Paved the Way

Marlene O'Bryant Seabrook l Charleston, North Carolina l 2008 l 35 x 38 inches (89 x 97 cm) l African and commercial fabrics, gold Etal (real metal on flexible substrate) textile paint, African bone beads, and cowrie shells l Photo transfer; painted; machine appliquéd, pieced, and quilted l *Photo by Chas. E. and Mary B. Martin*

Marlene O'Bryant Seabrook

They Paved the Way

The road that led to Barack Obama becoming the forty-fourth president of the United States of America was paved by many persons and events focused on bringing to fruition America's promise that "all men are created equal." On the evening of November 4, 2008, like others all over America—and abroad—I was glued to my television set. I was prepared to watch the returns until the wee hours of the morning and was stunned when around midnight, it was announced that Barack Obama had 338 electoral votes—well over the 270 needed—and he was declared the winner. This young African American man had just become our president. I was elated, overwhelmed, speechless! Having been born in the thirties, I could not help but remember the indignities of Jim Crow and the sacrifices of the civil rights movement. I could not help but think that our president-elect was standing firmly on the shoulders of many who had paved the way for him.

I went to sleep knowing that there was a quilt in there somewhere, and in the next few days brainstormed sixty-seven names and events. As they often do, my quilt design came during my dreams—a path of engraved "bricks" led to a portrait of our president. When I was invited to create one of forty-four quilts for an inaugural exhibition at the Historical Society of Washington, DC, I decided to concentrate on the civil rights era and limit my bricks to forty-four. Several of my original ideas were covered by the inclusion of four organizations.

The quilt features forty-four gold stepping stones that are symbolic of the precious lives, blood, sweat, and tears of those named and, vicariously, of others unnamed and unknown. All gave some, but the first six rows and the collage at the top honor those who gave ALL. I chose the African fabric with the cowrie-shell print because it is doubly significant. It recognizes President Obama's paternal heritage, as well as the fact that until 1807, the British used cowrie shells as currency to purchase so many of the ancestors who never could have imagined this historic milestone. The thirteen gold-painted cowrie shells attached at the bottom represent the history of the thirteen original colonies from 1619 to 1865.

Rows:

1. Emmett Till, Sixteenth Street Baptist Church bombing, Addie Mae Collins

2. Denise McNair, Cynthia Wesley, Carole Robertson

3. Andrew Goodman, Michael Schwerner, James Chaney

4. Malcolm X, Medgar Evers, Viola Liuzzo

5. Samuel Hammond, Delano Middleton, Henry Smith

6. Orangeburg Massacre, Martin Luther King Jr., Martin Luther King Jr. assassination

7. NAACP (National Association for the Advancement of Colored People), SCLC (Southern Christian Leadership Conference), SNCC (Southern Nonviolent Coordinating Committee), CORE (Congress of Racial Equality)

8. Coretta Scott King, Andrew Young, Ralph Abernathy, John Lewis

9. Thurgood Marshall, *Brown v. Board of Education*, Central High School desegregation, James Meredith

10. Rosa Parks, Montgomery Bus Boycott, lunch counter sit-ins, Freedom Marchers

11. March on Washington, Fannie Lou Hamer, Freedom Riders, Septima P. Clark, Selma-to-Montgomery march

12. Voting Rights Act, Executive Order 11246 (affirmative action), Jesse Jackson, Cleveland Sellers, Civil Rights Acts of 1964 and 1968

Latifah Shakir
Dream the Impossible Dream

I treated this quilt as a canvas, expressing my abstract composition in colors and forms, using red, white, and blue strips of recycled materials with added embellishments. I also integrated pointed stars around the quilt and painted it to unite the union. My crazy quilting journey with Barack Obama was exhilarating and fascinating to say the least. The red fabrics stood for the red states, the blue fabrics stood for the blue states, and, as President Obama so eloquently expressed in his speeches, we are rightly known as the United States. The decorative threads and yarn represent the many roads he traveled all over the country. The buttons symbolize crowds of people gathering in stadiums and arenas to see and hear him speak. Recycled grocery bags and netted plastic sacks symbolize the poor economy and high price of food. The large zipper in the center of the quilt represents the men of the campaign trail. The small zipper and bra straps represent the women on the campaign trail. Lastly, the hands on the back of the quilt stand for all the handshakes of people and waving to crowds from town to town. The house represents homes he visited on the trail. With this abstract composition, each viewer interprets differently his or her own meaning.

I experienced excitement, frustration, highs, and lows during the election of 2008; however, it was worth it. The making of this quilt will live with me forever.

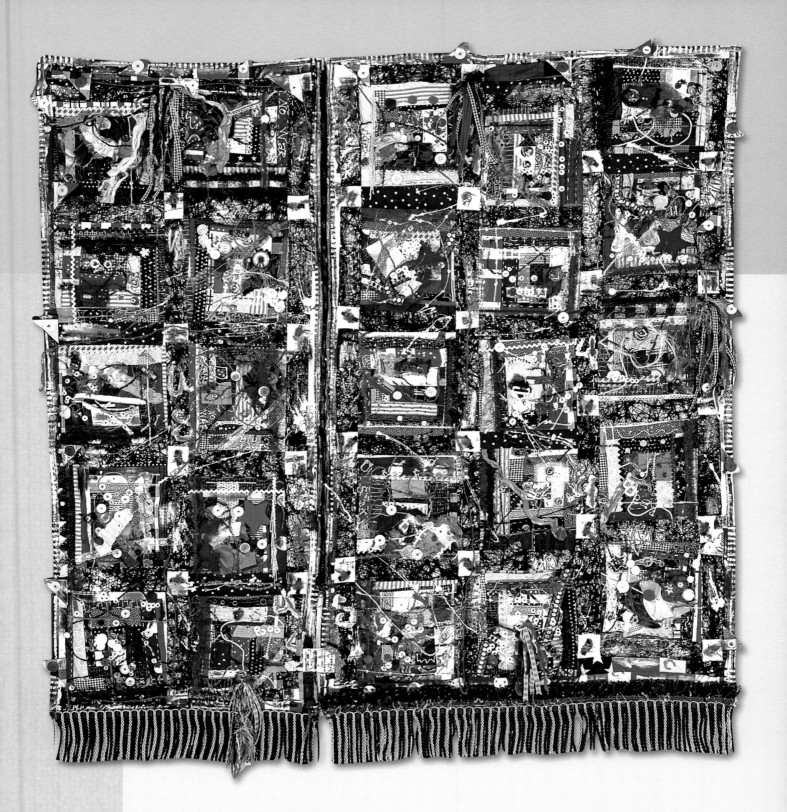

Dream the Impossible Dream

Latifah Shakir I Lawrenceville, Georgia I 2009 I 64 x 60.5 inches (163 x 194 cm) I Recycled fabrics, paint,
buttons, beads, plastic bags I Hand and machine sewn, couched I *Photo by Chas. E. and Mary B. Martin*

War and Freedom: African American Veterans Hail the Commander in Chief #2

Carole Lyles Shaw I Columbia, Maryland I 2009 I 36 x 41 inches (91 x 104 cm) I Cottons, acrylic paints I Photo transfer, painted, and idiosyncratic machine quilted I *Photo by Chas. E. and Mary B. Martin.*

Carole Lyles Shaw

War and Freedom:
African American Veterans Hail the Commander in Chief #2

My Obama art quilts are from a major series titled War, Honor and Freedom that I started in 2006. The War, Honor and Freedom works are mixed-media collages, assemblages, and art quilts that document the lives of ordinary men and women who served in the U.S. military, with a particular focus on the early twentieth century. I started this series with mixed-media collages that honored my father and uncles, who were World War II and Korean War veterans. As I searched through family photos and memorabilia, I was struck by the paradox of their honorable service in the fight against tyranny and evil during a period when their civil rights were legally curtailed by Jim Crow, segregation, and social customs. In fact, during this period, these soldiers could have been lynched for daring to vote or deciding to eat at a whites-only diner. Although few African American women served, they shared this experience, and their story is even less well known, so I highlight their service as well.

I began collecting additional material from friends and relatives, and from the "world's flea market," otherwise known as eBay. I collected photos, letters, uniforms, and other memorabilia of both identified and unidentified veterans of all races, both male and female, from the first half of the twentieth century. President Obama plays many roles, and one of them is commander in chief of the armed forces of the United States. When President Obama was elected, I knew that these veterans—whether they were still living or with us only in spirit—would have served proudly under the newly elected commander in chief. In the Obama works, I always include a copy of my own ballot, quotes from the Constitution, and election and inauguration memorabilia.

Maria C. Shell

Colors Unfurled
(aka If Betsy Ross Had My Stash)

Patriot: *one who supports and defends one's country.*

During the Bush administration, the word *patriot* was narrowly defined to represent a certain type of American. President George Bush's mantra was, "Either you are with us, or you are with the terrorists." The symbol of this patriotism was the American flag. We were encouraged to wear the flag and blindly follow. To question was unpatriotic; to challenge was un-American.

During the buildup to the Iraq War, my mother bought my three sons several American flag T-shirts. I gave them to Goodwill. I could not let my children wear the American flag when doing so was tacit support for an unnecessary war—a war they might have to fight.

I love my country. I am a patriot. But in the McCarthyesque environment created by the Bush administration, I felt silenced.

And then an amazing thing happened. Barack Obama announced his run for the presidency. As I watched the race in all its twists and turns, I witnessed the unbelievable. I saw a country transforming itself. During the Democratic Convention, I started stitching a new version of the American flag. My quilt, *Colors Unfurled (aka If Betsy Ross Had My Stash)*, is an act of reclaiming *patriotism* and the American flag as a word and a symbol that belong to ALL of us.

Techniques used in *Colors Unfurled* include freeform piecing and thread play. Traditional quilting cottons from the 1920s to the present day, as well as many ethnic fabrics, are joined together to celebrate the great diversity of America, to shout with joy that we are at a wonderful moment in our history.

America is many colors, many classes, many cultures, and many communities, and they all have something to say. May we listen to each other with respect and love. May we have the courage to follow our new president and the tenacity to change.

Colors Unfurled (aka If Betsy Ross Had My Stash)

Maria C. Shell I Anchorage, Alaska I 2009 I 77 x 126 inches (196 x 320 cm) I Vintage and
contemporary cotton fabrics, extensive thread play I Freeform quilt construction inspired
by traditional patchwork I *Photo by Chris Arend*

Susan Shie

First Lady

I see my narrative art quilts as visual time capsules. Usually I multitask them. Having made many large pieces about Barack Obama, this time I wanted to make something all about Michelle Obama, but it's also my second piece in the Minor Arcana in my Kitchen Tarot quilt project. (I finished the twenty-two Major Arcana card quilts last year, having started the project in 1998. There are fifty-six minor cards—lots of Obamas to go!)

Like our new first lady, the Queen of Swords card stands for a very intelligent and hard-working woman who mentors others. She has learned a lot of lessons in life, which she passes on in her wisdom. In my Kitchen Tarot deck, the sword cards become paring knives. Not weapons but helpful tools.

I airbrushed Michelle holding a vase of my Peace Roses. Barack is next to her, also holding the vase, and the girls, Malia and Sasha, stand in front of Michelle. I made her flashing the "shaka" sign, and I wrote "First Lady" on the bodice of her gown.

The pies are my symbols of gifts and blessings. The many faces in the background are both men and women, black people who are rallying behind the Obamas, having voted for Barack and now hoping for the best for the first African American president and his family.

I transcribed a few important items onto this piece, including all of Michelle's speech at the 2008 Democratic Convention and Barack's letter to his daughters, which he published in *Parade* magazine just prior to his inauguration. But mostly my writing here includes my own diary entries, which range from deaths in my family to journalist Roxana Saberi's hostage release in Iran. Oh, and Wanda Sykes' speech at the White House Correspondents' Dinner. I liked that!

First Lady

Susan Shie l Wooster, Ohio l 2009 l 93 x 83 inches (236 x 211 cm) l Whole cloth painting on white cloth, fabric paint, cotton prints for backing cloth, Nature-fil bamboo and cotton batting, machine thread, perle cotton thread, Buddha beads l Airbrushed, painted with fabric paint, drawn with air pen and fabric paint, machine quilted l *Photo by artist*

Sherry Shine

Chronicles of a Journey

This quilt is a collaged documentation of pieces of our history woven into fabric. It touches upon the evolution of African Americans and the important roles they have played throughout American history. A pathway was created by our ancestors to guide us in the right direction and move us forward to witness the election of the first African American president of the United States of America.

Though African American history has been filled with cruelty, history is constantly being reshaped, and we have never given up hope. We could not have accomplished all we have without making tough choices. There are those who stood in the face of adversity and had faith that African Americans could overcome. *Chronicles of a Journey* was developed with this in mind. Pieces of the quilt were hand drawn and painted using acrylics. I also used appliqué, picture transfers, and transcribed text. With the addition of each layer, I was reminded of our struggles and all we have overcome. This quilt is a reflection of and a tribute to those whose battles have been won and lost in the name of freedom and equality. It encompasses the past to remind us of what promise the future can bring. A journey that is not yet complete. A new chronicle must be completed with the realization that "we" are all connected and "Yes We Can" accomplish anything.

Chronicles of a Journey

Sherry Shine I East Orange, New Jersey I 2008 I 52 x 52 inches (132 x 132 cm) I Mixed media, collage using photographs, and fabric paint I Quilted by Rebecca Segura I *Photo by Chas. E. and Mary B. Martin*

Sherry Shine
Fearless

Rosa Parks and President Barack Obama are two iconic figures who changed the face of history with the understanding that greatness is never given—it must be earned. Each of these icons stands for the "journey of hope" in all of us and is connected through the many challenges we have faced. Their persistence, courage, and optimism have proved that progress continues to be made and we all have an obligation to stand up for what we believe in.

Fearless

Sherry Shine I East Orange, New Jersey I 2009 I 36 x 46 inches (91 x 117 cm) I Fabric
paint and charcoal pencil on whole cloth cotton I *Photo by Chas. E. and Mary B. Martin*

***The 44th* was based on a speech** that I saw President Obama give when he was running for office. This particular quilt has a lot of symbolism and metaphors. His image is done in black, white, and gray to address the issue of race relations in this country. The quilt stands for what he spoke about in his speech, which is not whether we are black or white but that we are all Americans and we each have to contribute to making this country that we live in a better place for everyone.

The 44th

Sherry Shine Ι East Orange, New Jersey Ι 2009 Ι 27 x 25 inches (69 x 64 cm) Ι Fabric paint and charcoal pencil on whole cloth Ι Quilted by Olga Butora Ι *Photo by Chas. E. and Mary B. Martin*

Penny Sisto

Obamessiah

My quilt represents the concept of Barack Obama as savior— political savior. The flowers in his hand symbolize peace, because I believe him to be a man of peace. The enslaved African symbolizes the history of the slave trade in America. Icons who impacted American history by affecting the condition of African Americans are symbolized by Abraham Lincoln, who is much admired by President Obama; Harriet Tubman; and Dr. Martin Luther King Jr. Flaming embers fall around President Obama. However, they don't touch him. He is protected by the prayers of many who pray daily for his safety and strength during his tenure as president of the United States.

Obamessiah

Penny Sisto I Floyd Knobs, Indiana I 2009 I 44 x 36 inches (112 x 91 cm) I Cotton, acrylic paint, metallic fabric I Hand embellished, machine appliquéd, and machine quilted I *Photo by Chas. E. and Mary B. Martin*

Bonnie J. Smith

Obama in Blue

I, like most Americans, had been following the 2008 presidential election very closely. I was elated when Barack Obama won the presidency. At our house, we popped the cork on a bottle of champagne and said, "New days are coming." Knowing full well what a historical day in my life and in the entire world this was, I couldn't believe I was alive to witness this moment in time. It was as if the United States of America had finally started on the road to becoming a mature country.

I used the face of President Barack Obama over and over, hoping everyone would get the message "He is our president, and I am proud." Mr. Barack Obama is now officially president of the United States of America, and with each passing day, I know we have the right leader who is leading us to our full potential as human beings.

Obama in Blue

Bonnie J. Smith I San Jose, California I 2008 I 40 x 40 inches (102 x 102 cm) I Cotton, polyester thread, fabric paint, polyester batting I Screen printed, machine quilted, hand-sewn binding I *Photo by artist*

Louisa Smith
Yes We Can

As an immigrant (I became a citizen on April 15, 1968), the election of 2008 gave me a sense of hope for the future. I just had to re-create an image of what we were seeing on the newsstands around the country and commemorate this milestone in American history. I cannot tell you how delighted I was. My relatives in Europe have that same feeling of joy. My relatives feel Obama is good for the United States, and what's good for the United States is good for the world!

Yes We Can

Louisa Smith I Loveland, Colorado I 2008 I 17 x 20.5 inches (43 x 52 cm) I Hand-dyed and commercial fabrics I Fused, machine appliquéd and quilted, embellished with hand stitching I *Photo courtesy of the Morris and Gwendolyn Cafritz Foundation Art Center*

Jim Smoote
Obama 44

Obama 44 is inspired by a photograph of Barack H. Obama. This quilt was envisioned as a contemporary take on traditional patchwork. The composition combines forty-four multicolored machine-pieced patches, hand appliquéd with forty-four ink-jet prints on cotton, embellished with acrylic paint. In the center is an appliquéd panel of the Obama logo.

Obama 44

Jim Smoote I Chicago, Illinois I 2008 I 48 x 48 inches (122 x 122 cm) I Acrylic on ink-jet print, assorted fabrics I Hand appliquéd and quilted, machine pieced I *Photo by Chas. E. and Mary B. Martin*

Inspired Change

Carole Gary Staples I West Chester, Ohio I 2008 I 36 x 36 inches (91 x 91 cm) I Cotton batik I Paper pieced, appliquéd, machine quilted I *Photo by Chas. E. and Mary B. Martin*

Carole Gary Staples
Inspired Change

For me, 2008 was an inspiring year. It was a year that witnessed historic changes large and small. This quilt is the manifestation of the metamorphosis that I and many Americans experienced. As we listened to the candidates present their platforms, Barack Obama emerged as a strong leader with a new, refreshing outlook and message. He spoke of change, hope, and inclusion. His message was different from the "same old thing" presented another way. He inspired a nation with his confidence, courage, and strength to be different.

In 2008, I was inspired and began to hope. I experienced a complete political metamorphosis. I changed from being a member of the Republican Party to a member of the Democratic Party. I changed from being partially informed to being fully informed. I changed from being politically inactive to being an active campaign worker, canvassing the streets, working the phones of the phone banks, and attending events. I donated funds to a campaign for the very first time. I am proud to be one of the thousands of ordinary Americans who played a part in a historical election and a movement of change that was inspired by the forty-fourth president of the United States of America, Barack Hussein Obama.

Unparalleled Journey

Carole Gary Staples I West Chester, Ohio I 2009 I 36 x 36 inches (91 x 91 cm) I Cotton batik I Paper pieced, appliquéd, machine quilted I *Photo courtesy of the artist*

Carole Gary Staples
Unparalleled Journey

When I reflect upon the United States of America's journey to elect an African American as its forty-fourth president, my heart radiates with joy and astonishment. *Unparalleled Journey* commemorates images of many of the symbolic, authentic, and significant events encountered along this journey.

Quotations by Barack Obama and other historic leaders flank the outer border of the quilt. Many of the symbolic images within the piece reflect the meaning and prophecy of those quotations. The three ribbons of color, which flow through the work, represent three journeys, parallel in time yet unparalleled in reality.

Slavery The brown print fabric at the bottom of the piece represents the land this great country is built upon. Footprints dominate the green print. I chose to show those who survived the historic Middle Passage, and the blue print represents the water that delivered a people to the shores of this land. The female images depict the dark days of slavery. The figure clad in the muted-hued dress is a slave; the one in the vibrant dress is freed. Also celebrated are the old Negro hymns and the Emancipation Proclamation, without which this journey could never have been made.

Unity I've included a rainbow in my piece to signify that unity is possible among all Americans; it is representative of the multitude of ethnicities that make up this country. Mountains seen in the background reflect the strength required to continue on the journey and reflect the many references to mountains made by the Reverend Martin Luther King Jr. in his speeches. Any bill signed into law by the president of the United States requires paperwork and documentation, so I have included three blank documents as well to represent historic legislation such as *Brown v. Board of Education*, the Civil Rights Act, and the Voting Rights Act.

Diversity The autumn scenery in the background represents a figurative change of season in America. Diversity is represented in the rally of the diverse people seen on the face in the quilt. While we are different in many ways, we are all Americans and we have journeyed well together.

Maxine S. Thomas

Barack Obama: Realizing the American Dream

This quilt was inspired by the legal legacy that made it possible for Barack Obama, an African American lawyer, to ascend to the highest governmental post in America. From the shores of Africa to slavery in the United States, African Americans have waited on the legal promise of America to be realized. Obama was a constitutional lawyer steeped in the promise of the American dream. Constitutional amendments, laws, legal principles, hopes, dreams, and song are a part of this promise. The quilt includes samples of all these, as well as text from landmark decisions and events from the very earliest beginnings of the United States through the oath of office for the forty-fourth president.

As a lawyer, I am both inspired by how much of the American dream Barack Obama has been able to realize and cognizant of how much still remains to be accomplished for so many African Americans.

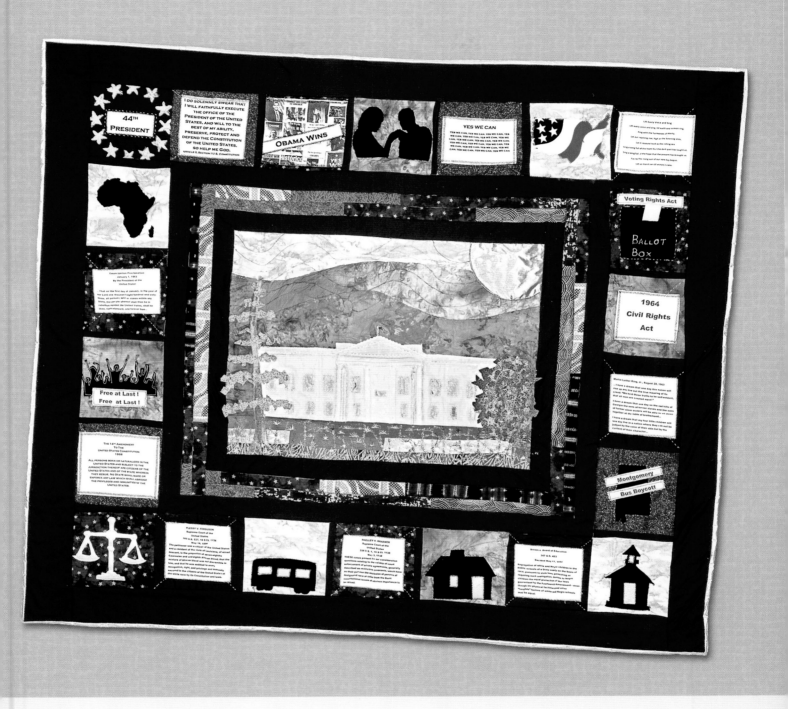

Barack Obama: *Realizing the American Dream*

Maxine S. Thomas I Jamestown, Ohio I 2009 I 42 x 42 inches (107 x 107 cm) I American and African cottons, batik fabric, hand-dyed fabrics I Appliquéd, painted, stenciled, machine and hand quilted, and hand embroidered I *Photo by Chas. E. and Mary B. Martin*

Rosalind Thomas
In My Time

In My Time travels through time, from slavery in the 1600s to the current day. My quilt takes the audience on a spiral historical journey from the plantation and the master's house through the cotton fields and a slave shanty; from a one-room dilapidated schoolhouse to institutions of higher learning, by the grace of God. Now, in the White House, African Americans continue to make strides in America.

In My Time

Rosalind Thomas I Hamilton, Ohio I 2009 I 36 x 36 inches (91 x 91 cm) I Whole cloth cotton I Hand painted with acrylic paint; quilted by artist and Moya Jones I *Photo by Chas. E. and Mary B. Martin*

Obama Equals Hope

Jeanette Thompson I Chicago, Illinois I 2008 I 24 x 24 inches (61 x 61 cm)
I Cotton I Machine appliquéd and quilted I *Photo courtesy of the artist*

Jeanette Thompson
Obama Equals Hope

It didn't take long for my husband and I to fall in love with Obama, especially as Election Day drew near. He offered hope and promised change with a calm demeanor that brought us comfort during a challenging time. My husband had been unemployed for more than twenty months, with little hope of finding a job in a worsening economy. Like many Americans, we were going through a tough time, struggling to keep our home and stay afloat, something that Obama seemed to understand.

As soon as Obama won the election, a feeling of dismay seemed to lift and be replaced with a new sense of hope. Just days later, I felt the need to make something to celebrate this special event. Inspiration first came from the familiar image of Obama's face designed by Shepard Fairey. I also felt the need to incorporate the word *hope* into the design. My husband suggested using the design of the *HOPE* sculpture that Robert Indiana made for the Democratic Convention. These two images were overlapped to create the quilt design. Next came fabric patterns and color choices to both emphasize images and challenge the viewer to see one image first, then discover the second image. I didn't want to use patriotic colors, like red, white, and blue. I wanted to use very bright, happy, and what I considered hopeful colors.

I showed the finished quilt to my high school art students, and they loved it. One class applauded with excitement. Knowing that we shared a common love for our future president was a special moment in time that I will never forget. This quilt is one of my favorite creations.

Elizabeth Warner
Together
We Bridge the Divide

I created two quilts in honor of the election of President Barack Obama.
His election was such a joyous, affirming, and, yes, emotional event in my life that the opportunity to create and display quilts that expressed some of my thoughts and feelings was welcomed and embraced.

I have always felt that, in this country, we have the capacity to create a just society. My firm belief is that President Obama can help us create the will to do and be better.

In recent years, our reputation throughout the world has declined, yet many continue to take great risks to come to our shores. The fact that our country has demonstrated to the world our ability to embrace President Obama and his family affirms that we continue to live in a land of hope and opportunity.

Together We Can Bridge the Divide illustrates four areas where the chasm between the haves and the have-nots is especially apparent. While I have no expectation that our elected officials can, with the magic of new legislation, make everything better, I do expect that, working together, government and the people—present in both secular and non-secular organizations dedicated to creating elements of a just society, as well as individuals who simply want to do the right thing—can move us forward.

Together We Can Bridge the Divide

Elizabeth Warner I Simsbury, Connecticut I 2008 I 28 x 28 inches (71 x 71 cm) I Domestic commercial fabrics; rayon, cotton, and polyester threads I Machine pieced and embroidered; machine quilted I *Photo by Mary Staley*

Torreah Cookie Washington

The Hope
of a New Day Begun

This quilt is about the new leaf of hope, held gently between two hands, which symbolizes all Americans. It is inspired by the words of our new president, Barack Obama: "There's not a black America and white America and Latino America and Asian America; there's the United States of America"; "This is our moment. This is our time."

On November 4, 2008, a night that symbolized a tremendous stride in our American journey, the words of James Weldon Johnson came to mind: "Sing a song full of the hope that the present has brought us."

The Hope of a New Day Begun

Torreah Cookie Washington | Charleston, South Carolina | 2008 | 36 inches (91 cm) in diameter | Cotton | Machine embroidered; hand and machine appliquéd and quilted | *Photo by Chas. E. and Mary B. Martin*

Valerie C. White

Great Expectations

Great Expectations

Valerie C. White I Louisville, Kentucky I 2008 I
31 x 31 inches (79 x 79 cm) I Textile paint, hand-dyed
cotton, cotton thread, hand-drawn appliquéd images,
laminated fabric I Machine quilted I *Photo by
Chas. E. and Mary B. Martin*

History was made on so many levels during the campaign and ultimately with the election of our forty-fourth president.

It was thrilling to see so many children attending campaign events accompanied by their parents. What an opportunity to teach our children to appreciate and develop a "Yes, we can" attitude.

Barack Obama is living proof that my sons, daughters, and grandchildren can, indeed, become president or anything else that may interest them. At last they can see someone whose reflection looks very much like their own and know that all goals are attainable, all things are possible!

Valerie C. White
In His Father's Village

Kogelo, Kenya, November 4, 2008

I will never stop thinking about the powerful images of the people in
Kogelo, Kenya, as they celebrated the election of President Barack Obama. The
unbridled spirit and compassion of the people were infectious. I found myself
dancing, laughing, and crying with them, but most of all wishing I could be there.
It was Africa, the cradle of civilization, "the Motherland"! It was the home of our
president's father! I wanted to exhale and embrace the moment forever.

I am blessed beyond measure to create a quilt that prayerfully captures the
essence of that extraordinary day. This work was produced to pay respect to
Barack Obama Sr. and the people of Kogelo, Kenya.

In His Father's Village

Valerie C. White | Louisville, Kentucky | 2009 | 22 x 22 inches (56 x 56 cm) | Textile paint, cotton fabric, cotton thread,
hand-drawn appliquéd images, artist-developed fax screen | Machine quilted | *Photo by Chas. E. and Mary B. Martin*

Cleota Wilbekin
Mama's Freedom Apron

This apron was made in honor of the African American domestic worker women who refused to ride the city bus in Montgomery, Alabama. The Montgomery Bus Boycott began on December 5, 1955, and lasted 381 days, ending after the U.S. Supreme Court ruled, on November 13, 1956, that segregation on public transportation was illegal and unconstitutional. During the boycott, routes were closed and the people sustained an abundance of violence. This successful boycott brought the bus company near bankruptcy because of these courageous people—who walked and walked and walked.

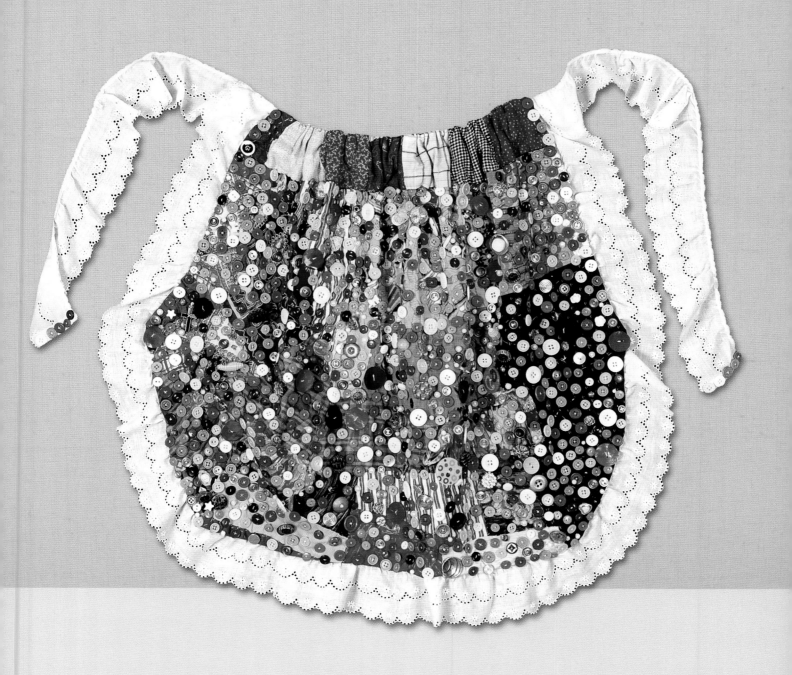

Mama's Freedom Apron

Cleota Wilbekin I Cincinnati, Ohio I 2008 I 26 x 24 inches (66 x 61 cm) I Antique patchwork, lace, buttons
I Hand pieced and quilted I *Photo by Chas. E. and Mary B. Martin*

6 Hours

My quilt *6 Hours* was inspired by the day I decided to vote early for the election.
I arrived at the poll at noon and did not leave until six o'clock. As I waited in line, I was
astounded by the number of voters in line, but more amazing were the stories that each one
had to tell. I met a young woman who had just lost her job and an elderly woman in a wheel-
chair who believed that this election would be monumental. Some voters stated that it was
an honor to be a part of history.

When I finally voted, I was given ticket number 595, and my heart skipped a beat. I could
not believe that almost six hundred voters and I were about to make history. As I exited the
building, I stated to a young woman who had voted after me that I could not believe we had
waited six hours to vote. We did not want to leave because it was so amazing—this long line
of people waiting to vote. As I sipped coffee to keep warm, I realized it was all worth the wait.
We even renamed the street Obama Avenue because everyone believed he was going to
win. Voting day began with voters like me waiting patiently for a dream to come true. It did
not matter that it was bitterly cold or that we had to wait so long. What really mattered is
that "we believed." *Belief* is a powerful word that can inspire people to make history. My vote
counted, along with those of other Americans who helped Obama deliver a dream that we
had all waited for, for a long time.

6 Hours

Sherise Marie Wright I Calumet City, Illinois I 2009 I 32.5 x 30 inches (83 x 76 cm) I Cotton, embroidery floss, fabric
paint, beads, faux fur I Machine appliquéd and quilted, hand embroidered, hand painted, and thread painted I *Photo
by Chas. E. and Mary B. Martin*

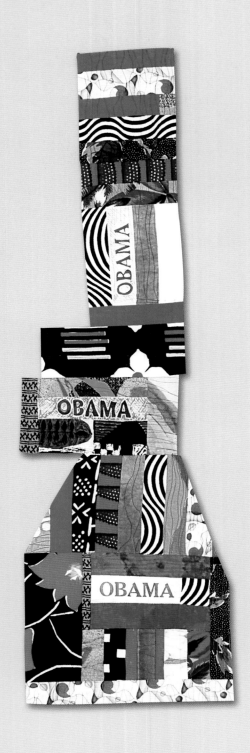

Obama

The only time I have used references to politicians in my work in the past has been in a negative way. When President Obama was elected, I was elated. I had felt so disenfranchised in the previous eight years that I had almost given up on the possibility that this country could elect a person of Mr. Obama's character. I hadn't planned on creating an Obama quilt; I just couldn't help myself. He is brilliant and calm and makes me proud to be an American.

Obama

Adrienne Yorinks I Short Hills, New Jersey I 2009 I 53 x 50 inches (135 x 127 cm) I Photo transfers, cotton, silk, blends, fabric pen I Machine pieced and quilted I *Photo by D. James Dee*

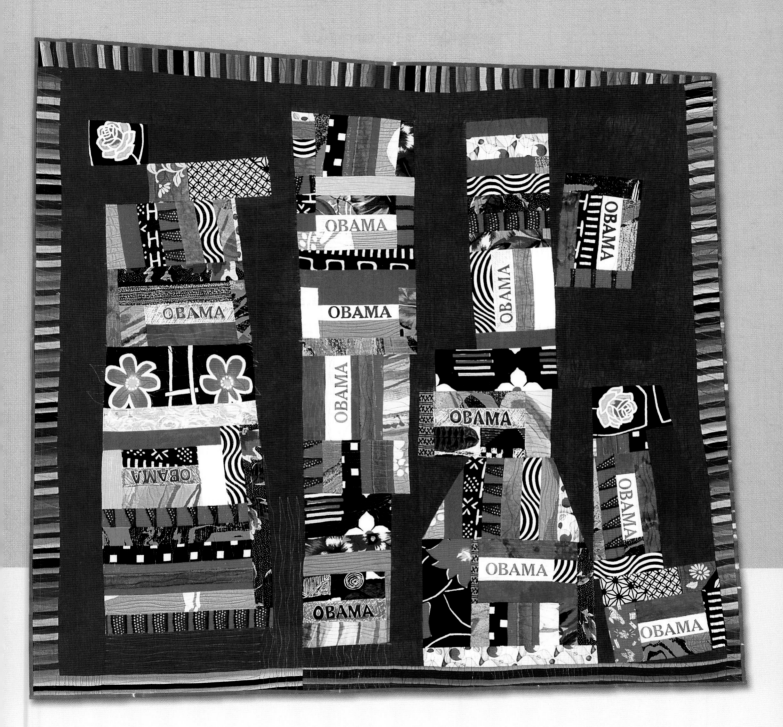

Keepers of Your Destiny

Sauda A. Zahra I Durham, North Carolina I 2008 I 34 x 34 inches (86 x 86 cm) I Cotton fabrics, photo transfer, hand embroidery I Machine pieced and hand quilted I *Photo by Chas. E. and Mary B. Martin*

Sauda A. Zahra

Keepers of Your Destiny

Many people's deeds and unyielding spirits have paved the way for the election of an African American as president of the United States. *Keepers of Your Destiny* celebrates this victory by reflecting on key historical events in the civil rights movement that helped illuminate a brighter path for Obama's journey toward shaping a new America.

The quilt speaks to the viewer in symbols that convey the significance of past contributions as a pathway to the future. The brick wall represents the overwhelming obstacles African Americans have confronted since arriving in this country. The missing bricks (green areas) illustrate the pivotal events occurring during the civil rights movement that helped knock down barriers in this country. The silhouette of Obama rising from the brick wall reminds us of the hope and faith many people held onto that one day an Obama would emerge. The footsteps leading to the White House contain names of people who were active during the civil rights movement. The footsteps honor others who contributed to making America more inclusive so that the possibility of an African American president could become a reality. The footsteps at the tip of the White House list the names of Obama's parents and grandparents in honor of their impact on his life. A small skeleton key at their feet symbolizes that their spirits will be with him as he enters the White House. Africa placed in the sun acknowledges Obama's direct lineage, the descendents of slaves in this country, and the worldwide impact of his election. The background for the quilt is made from a quilt block pattern called Road to the White House, which was designed and named by the *Farm Journal* in January 1938. It seemed appropriate to use this design as a backdrop for the quilt.

Si se Puede! Dancing at the Revolution

Sabrina Zarco I Little Rock, Arkansas I 2009 I 61 x 60 inches (155 x 152 cm) I Altered commercial fabric, computer-generated fabric, thread, paint, beads, netting, and buttons I Hand and machine quilted, raw-edge appliquéd, embroidered, painted, and beaded I *Photo by Chas. E. and Mary B. Martin*

Sabrina Zarco

Si se Puede!
Dancing at the Revolution

As a Latina artist-activist, I visually journal my walk with marginalized communities by documenting stories overlooked by mainstream media. Preserving stories and promoting civic dialogue can lead to authentic connections with one another. It can facilitate a healing for our generational wounds and serve as a tool for personal and community empowerment. The fight for social justice takes place in all arenas, and art, a unifying language, has always been a part of change for communities of color.

Emma Goldman's saying "If I can't dance, I don't want to be part of your revolution" is one source of inspiration for this work. It explores the celebratory dimensions as change agents, community activists, and organizers. The tree of *esperanza* (hope) in this work grows leaves of words: *equality*, *dignity*, *solidarity*, *vision*, *compassion*, and *love*. This work commemorates community organizers and activists. Some came before us, paving the way, and others continue the work, all sharing the vision of *Si se puede* (Yes we can). Names of these change agents, such as Dolores Huerta, Gloria Anzaldua, Harvey Milk, Coretta Scott King, and President Obama, are recognized on this piece. Obama began his career as a community organizer and continues to be an agent of change.

> "One of my fundamental beliefs from my days as a community organizer is that real change comes from the bottom up."
>
> —*President Barack Obama.*

Kathy Zieben
Waves of Change

new and better way

"Times change and we change with them."

—*Latin proverb*

America's first black president, Barack Obama, will modify history and hopefully take the United States in a new, better direction. This is my hope for our country in the next four years!

My inspiration for this quilt came from using two different images of Obama's face. Having two faces— one looking to the future and one to the past—allows Barack Obama to build a strong foundation on his current knowledge and build layers of change from the experiences he will encounter in the next four years. I chose to layer the images and frame them with "waves of change" for the future.

My dream is that my quilt will inspire people to go after what they want and that change can bring about new direction! President Barack Obama's victory has demonstrated that anyone, anywhere in the world, can dream of wanting to change the world.

One nation under God, indivisible, with liberty and justice for all.

Waves of Change

Kathy Zieben I Sugar Land, Texas I 2008 I 14 x 22 inches (36 x 56 cm) I Used clothing, new fabrics, threads, cotton batting, scanned and superimposed images I
Photo by artist

Acknowledgments

This book would have been impossible without the talent of the quilt artists who so generously contributed images to this book. A special thanks to my dear sisterfriend, Marla Jackson, who was always close by with her wit and humor when this project became frustrating. Special thanks to Dr. Myrah Green, my resident griot, who keeps the memory of the ancestors at the forefront of all we do. My thanks to the Women of Color Quilters Network who have always been so generous with their talents, and continue to record the history of our people in cloth. All of you are amazing.

My thanks to my editor, Margret Aldrich, for her sensitivity to the words written by the makers of the quilts in *Journey of Hope*.

I am profoundly indebted to Dr. Denise Campbell and L'Merchie Fraizer for their support and belief that my work is important. To Chas. E. and Mary Martin, thank you for your photography and design work.

Special thanks to the staff at the National Afro-American Museum and Cultural Center for organizing the *Journey of Hope* touring exhibition. I especially thank Edna Diggs for keeping up with all the paperwork and Wendy Felder for facilitating the shipping of the quilts to Yokohama, Japan. I am appreciative of the enthusiasm and passion you both have for quilts.

I reserve special thanks for my husband Rezvan Mazloomi, the most spiritual being I've ever known, for his love and support.

Finally, I give thanks to the ancestors who walk this journey with me.

About the Author

Carolyn L. Mazloomi is one of the world's most influential African American quilt historians and quilting artists. Her quilts are in numerous private, corporate, and museum collections, including the Smithsonian American Art Museum, the American Museum of Design, and the National Underground Railroad Freedom Center Museum. In 1985, Dr. Mazloomi founded the Women of Color Quilters Network, a major force in fostering quiltmaking in the African American community. Dr. Mazloomi is the author of several books, including *Spirits of the Cloth* and *Threads of Faith*, and she has curated many quilt exhibits, both nationally and internationally. She lives in West Chester, Ohio.